THE NATURE AND EFFECTIVENESS
OF BILINGUAL EDUCATION PROGRAMS
FOR THE SPANISH-SPEAKING CHILD
IN THE UNITED STATES

BILINGUAL-BICULTURAL EDUCATION
IN THE UNITED STATES

*See last pages of this volume
for a complete list of titles.*

THE NATURE AND EFFECTIVENESS OF BILINGUAL EDUCATION PROGRAMS FOR THE SPANISH-SPEAKING CHILD IN THE UNITED STATES

Solomon Hernández Flores

ARNO PRESS
A New York Times Company
New York • 1978

Editorial Supervision: LUCILLE MAIORCA

———◆———

First publication 1978 by Arno Press Inc.

Copyright © 1970 by Solomon Hernandez Flores

BILINGUAL-BICULTURAL EDUCATION IN THE UNITED STATES
ISBN for complete set: 0-405-11071-5
See last pages of this volume for titles.

Manufactured in the United States of America

———◆———

Library of Congress Cataloging in Publication Data

Flores, Solomon Hernández.
    The nature and effectiveness of bilingual education
programs for the Spanish-speaking child in the United
States.

    (Bilingual-bicultural education in the United States)
    Originally presented as the author's thesis, Ohio
State University, 1969.
    Bibliography: p.
    1. Education, Bilingual--United States.
2. Spanish-Americans--Education--United States.
I. Title. II. Series.
LC3731.F58 1978   371.9'7'6873   77-92296
ISBN 0-405-11082-0

THE NATURE AND EFFECTIVENESS OF BILINGUAL EDUCATION

PROGRAMS FOR THE SPANISH-SPEAKING

CHILD IN THE UNITED STATES

DISSERTATION

Presented in Partial Fulfillment of the Requirements for
the Degree Doctor of Philosophy in the Graduate
School of The Ohio State University

By

Solomon Hernández Flores, B.A., M.A.

* * * * * *

The Ohio State University
1969

ACKNOWLEDGMENTS

This study would not have been possible without the guidance, counsel, and encouragement of my reading committee consisting of my program adviser Dr. Edward D. Allen, Dr. Frank Otto, and Dr. Herbert L. Coon. To them I am deeply grateful for the time that they took from busy schedules to guide my work.

Many school administrators, teachers, and aides contributed to this study by sending me materials and offering helpful suggestions. I am especially grateful to the five elementary school principals who permitted me to visit their bilingual programs and to examine them critically. These principals are the following: Hernán LaFontaine, Public School Number 25, The Bilingual School, Bronx, New York; J. Lee Logan, Coral Way Elementary School, Miami, Florida; R. J. Waddell, Garfield Elementary School, Del Rio, Texas; Elías Herrera, Nye Elementary School, Laredo, Texas; and Rubén Sierra, J. T. Brackenridge Elementary School, San Antonio, Texas.

Every attempt has been made to give credit to the ideas and materials used or cited in this study. My position has been that of an interested researcher who has seen

ii

the need for a descriptive treatise on the nature and effectiveness of bilingual education programs for the Spanish-speaking child in the United States.

To my wife Maria Dolores, I express my thanks for her patience and understanding throughout my entire doctoral program. She has been a source of constant encouragement.

VITA

October 14, 1928 . . . . Born – Kansas City, Kansas

1953 . . . . B.A., Ottawa University, Ottawa,
Kansas

1956–1958 . . . . . . Teacher of English and Spanish,
Humboldt High School, Humboldt,
Kansas

1958–1964 . . . . . . Teacher of Spanish, Public Schools,
Kansas City, Missouri

1963 . . . . M.A., The University of Kansas,
Lawrence, Kansas

1964–1966 . . . . . . Instructor of Spanish, Northeastern
Illinois State College, Chicago,
Illinois

1966–1967 . . . . . . Graduate Student, The Ohio State
University, Columbus, Ohio

1967–1969 . . . . . . Teaching Associate, Department of
Romance Languages, The Ohio State
University, Columbus, Ohio

PUBLICATIONS

(Production Team) Curriculum Guide for Spanish, Levels I-
IV. Bulletin No. 143, Public Schools, Kansas City,
Missouri, Spring, 1963.

FIELDS OF STUDY

Major Field: Foreign Language Education

Studies in Foreign Language Education. Professors
Edward D. Allen, Paul Pimsleur, and Frank Otto

Studies in Teacher Education. Professors Leonard O.
Andrews, Herbert L. Coon, and Donald P. Cottrell

Studies in Audio-Visual Education. Professors I. Keith
Tyler, Edgar Dale, Robert Wagner, and Theodore Niel-
son

TABLE OF CONTENTS

CHAPTER I

INTRODUCTION

Background

Our public school philosophy is based on the
assumption that education is not the sole responsibility
of parents but that at a certain point society, or rather
its agencies, must step in and take over some of the task
of educating its members. /This being the case, it is
important to examine to what extent schools realize this
aim, especially since in many cases the Spanish-speaking
home situation of a sizeable percentage of our students
does not prepare them for adequate functioning in our
society.\ That this is a problem of great magnitude is
evidenced by the amount of interest currently present in
bilingual education, the inner-city of the Spanish-speaking,
and more recently, the enactment of the Bilingual Education
Act of 1967.

Dr. Albar Peña, Program Advisor, Bilingual Education
Section, U.S. Office of Education, recently pointed out
that 311 proposals were submitted to his office for funding
under the Bilingual Education Act of 1967. Eighty-one of
these proposals have been tentatively accepted and will

1

become operative in the fall of 1969. These new programs will increase the present number of "real" bilingual projects from twelve to ninety-three.[1]

The Mexican-American minority has received little attention from the mass media of communication and, outside the Southwest, California, and several large cities, there is hardly any awareness of its existence. This merits some thought since Mexican-Americans constitute the second largest minority in the United States. Added to this large concentration of Mexican-Americans are others in different parts of the United States, especially in the large cities, and even in small cities such as Topeka, Kansas, and Galesburg, Illinois. The other ethnic groups swell the total of Spanish-speaking people to over seven million: the Cubans, fleeing the Fidel Castro regime; and the ever-increasing number of Puerto Ricans, who continue to come to the United States. All of these ethnic groups present a really serious problem to the American educator.

Now, after many years of neglect and apathy, speakers of non-English languages in the United States have become objects of more positive attention. Attitudes are beginning to change, although slowly. These non-English speakers are now more frequently viewed as commanding a gift, a skill which has suddenly become a valuable asset for the country and, therefore, for themselves as individuals.

This has not been the case until recently although bilingual education has existed for centuries in different parts of the world as well as in the United States. The need for recognizing the bilingual child as a positive force in our society is beyond question. For this reason, it is ironic that in the Southwest some elementary schools have forbidden children to speak Spanish. At the same time we give lip service to the wisdom of learning foreign languages, and our government spends millions of dollars supporting programs whose aim it is to teach foreign languages to monolingual English-speaking students in high school and college. It is interesting to note that Spanish is one of the more popular electives.

The authors of the Northeast Conference Report on the Teaching of Foreign Languages, 1965 came to grips with the problem and expressed themselves in the following manner:

> There is a multi-million-pupil question at the American educator's door, to which the times at last are demanding an answer. Bluntly put, it is this: in view of our country's need for citizens highly competent in foreign languages, why does virtually no part of the effort and money go to develop and maintain the competence of those 19,000,000--children and adults--who already speak the languages natively? Why is it our public policy to ignore or stamp out the native competence while at the same time undertaking the miracle of creating something like it in our monolinguals?[2]

According to these educators, the time was at hand, national attitudes were favorable, and funds were available to develop and utilize the non-English resources of American ethnic groups. Also, they considered especially favorable the national climate for establishing more and better programs of bilingual education for the bilingual children of the United States. Great importance was given to the task of making these ethnic groups broadly literate in the non-English mother tongue. The foreign language profession was made to feel that it could no longer shirk this duty.

Briefly, the Conference agenda had as its main concern a three-fold approach: (1) developing the non-English mother tongue for its powerful integrative effect on the child's personality, (2) developing it as an adjunct to education and a career, and (3) developing it as a national resource. A fourth concern—developing bilinguals as a source of foreign language teachers—really pertained to foreign language teaching in the usual sense.[3]

At this point it is appropriate to point out what bilingual education is and where it fits into the whole of inner-city studies to which it is related. The reason for this is that bilingual children of a Spanish-speaking background are usually socially, economically, and linguistically handicapped in much the same way as the poor white and Negro children of the big cities in the United States. Quite often the only difference between the two groups is that of geography. Both groups share similar conditions of cultural disadvantageousness.

Mildred Boyer believes that there are in the United States many programs that are called bilingual, but that the labels are often misleading. While there is no intent to deceive, the term simply lends itself to confusion. She further points out that most so-called bilingual programs are programs _for_ bilinguals, not the programs themselves.[4] The language of the Bilingual Education Act, however, is clear on this point:

> Bilingual education is instruction in two languages and the use of those two languages as mediums of instruction for any part or all of the school curriculum. Study of the history and culture associated with a student's mother tongue is considered an integral part of bilingual education.[5]

A. Bruce Gaarder, one of the most prolific writers in the area of bilingual education and currently a Specialist in Foreign Languages, U.S. Office of Education, takes the following stand:

> A _bilingual_ school is a school which uses, concurrently, two languages as mediums of instruction in any portion of the curriculum except the languages themselves. Thus, for example, arithmetic in English and history in Irish, or all subjects (except Irish and English) in both tongues would constitute bilingual schooling. English through English and all other subjects in Irish would not. The teaching of a vernacular solely as a bridge to another, the official language, is not bilingual education in the sense of this paper, nor is ordinary foreign language teaching.[6]

Gaarder refers here to a "real" bilingual program as contrasted with those that are "transitional." The transitional program is the one utilized in some emerging country where one or more native languages are used in the primary grades, not out of any interest in bilingual education as such, but only as a concession to current difficulties in the schools. Thus, English as a Second Language, Teaching English to Speakers of Other Languages, Spanish for the Spanish-Speaking, all of these programs, are merely part of a greater whole--"real" bilingual education. A detailed description of operational models and strategies will be presented in Chapter III in which an attempt will be made to synthesize current thinking about what bilingual education really is.

Scope

The purpose of this study is to identify operational models and strategies presently being used in bilingual education programs. As no one single work is currently available on this subject, one of the aims of this study will be to examine the literature that does exist, most of which appears in pamphlets, articles, and other minor treatises. An attempt will be made to fully examine models and strategies from a theoretical basis as only a few appear to exist at the present time. In its most general form this study, then, will lay forth the theoretical bases of bilingual education and examine in depth several on-going programs to determine where theory and application meet.

Limitations of the Study

This study will be limited to considering the bilingual programs now in operation for the Spanish-speaking, whether these programs be for Mexican-Americans, Cubans, or Puerto Ricans. Ideally, the scope of this intended study should have provided for all bilingual education programs including, perhaps, those designed for American Indians and Franco-Americans. However, this study will be limited to an in-depth examination of five well established elementary programs and to a general survey of others. An attempt will be made to synthesize all data into an informative, up-to-date set of guidelines for successful bilingual education programs.

Review of the Literature

One general purpose of this study is to gather in one place as much information as possible about bilingual education as it pertains to the Spanish-speaking populace. Since 1965 several projects have been initiated, most of which were set up without specific guidelines available. Only now is there an attempt being made to look at these programs with a critical eye. Chapter II of this study is devoted to a detailed consideration of this literature.

Statement of the Problem

A preliminary investigation of the existing literature on bilingual education reflects a variety of ideas
about the aims and objectives of the components of a good,
adequate program for any one ethnic group. The writer
contacted state foreign language coordinators, city consultants, and prominent persons in the field of bilingual
education. Few of them were able to refer him to sources
that contained the rationale or criteria for their programs. As reflected in official correspondence from state
consultants of foreign languages in states such as Arizona,
New Jersey, Colorado, and Oklahoma, this fact is quite
evident. What this means is that many of the so-called
bilingual programs have developed mainly because funds
were available and plans had to be presented without
specific guidelines in mind. The reason for this, however,
is understandable as there were none to follow, and in
many cases some school systems could not count on the
advice of experts since there were few of them available
at the time. Lack of trained personnel, adequate materials, and adverse public opinion further complicated the
situation. Even those projects which undertook to provide
leadership and materials floundered somewhat in their
initial undertakings.

A good example of this type of endeavor is the
Foreign Language Innovative Curricula Studies (FLICS), a

Title III ESEA Project located at Ann Arbor, Michigan.
For the last two and a half years this project has provided
leadership in instructional materials for the teaching of
English as a second language and in conducting teacher
training programs on language and language teaching. In
part, the project was developed to meet the need for
teaching English to Spanish-speaking and other language-
handicapped children. The precise assessment of impact of
this program is difficult to determine, but effectiveness
can still be improved.

In a recent conference for Midwest Regional Directors of Migrant Education held in Lansing, Michigan, during
the summer of 1968, it was quite evident that no one person
was entirely aware of what was going on in areas out of
his immediate responsibility. The presence of a large
contingent of special consultants from the Texas Education
Agency further attested to the lack of qualified local
personnel to cope with the problems inherent in a bilingual
program. Teaching materials were also scarce and those
available were in a very early stage of development. The
main goals of the conference seemed to be those of sharing
information and of seeking some fundamental approaches to
initiating and carrying out successful programs of bilingual education.

The need for bilingual education is well established.
Men of prominence such as Wallace E. Lambert, Theodore

Andersson, Paul Bell, Ralph Robinett, and A. Bruce Gaarder
have clearly, and almost evangelistically, advocated this
curricular innovation. What is needed at this time is
some way of synthesizing the know-how of existent programs
in such a way that educators may have at their disposal
the fruits of available knowledge. It is to this end that
this study directs itself.

Bilingual education has passed the theoretical
point. We are now in the experimental stage, but the time
has come to eliminate the guesswork and to focus on the
underlying principles of curricular planning. Where
improvement is possible, research-based information must
be employed, theoretically at least, in the light of the
main objectives of the particular program in question.
With these assumptions set forth, the principal questions
to be answered in this study can thus be stated:

1. What are the criteria for establishing the
   best possible bilingual education programs for
   Spanish-speaking children?

2. How do present bilingual education programs
   measure up to these criteria?

3. What are some of the specific components of
   bilingual education that need to be strength-
   ened, minimized or modified?

Additional questions anticipated throughout the
course of this study relate to the following general areas:

1. Programs. Are the programs tailored to provide for the needs of the various ethnic groups

in the Spanish-speaking population (Mexican-
Americans, Cubans, and Puerto Ricans)?

2. Personnel. How are we meeting the need for
    supplying the new type of personnel for
    bilingual programs?

3. Curriculum. Are the materials now being
    used, linguistically and culturally oriented?
    Are American educators superimposing a "WASP"
    curriculum on the actual needs of the ethnic
    groups?

Three appendixes will provide a collection of data

and suggestions for integrating materials, teacher educa-

tion, and radio and television into bilingual programs.

CHAPTER II

REVIEW OF THE LITERATURE ON
BILINGUAL EDUCATION

The recent national interest in the disadvantaged
received its impetus from President Kennedy and was continued in high gear during the Johnson Administration.
As funds became available for projects for the disadvantaged in the ghettos of the cities, a new interest was
aroused in bilingual education for the bilingual disadvantaged. A national problem, long existent, finally
came to the fore and presented the American educator with
a unique challenge--that of providing not only special
education programs for the disadvantaged in the usual
sense, but also with the added dimension of providing
instruction via two languages, one the mother tongue and
the other, the second language. American educators had
long been aware of the situation in those areas where
Mexican-Americans live, mostly in the Southwest and
California, but had not come to grips with the problem
until the period of current national concern for the
welfare of its disadvantaged ethnic groups. The few programs in operation prior to 1960 were scattered throughout

12

the United States, and in most cases were isolated attempts
to keep alive a culture faced with complete absorption into
the American mainstream.

The Coral Way Elementary School in Miami, Florida,
made the most recent attempt to deal seriously with its
local ethnic problem. By 1963 the influx of refugees from
the Fidel Castro regime had altered the ethnic composition
in the neighborhood of this school. With a generous grant
from the Ford Foundation, the Dade County Board of Education set up a bilingual education program at the Coral Way
Elementary School. The nearly even number of Anglos and
Cubans was ideal for this type of venture. Since the
advent of this program, the national interest in this type
of school has picked up considerably. Enactment of the
Elementary and Secondary Education Act of 1965 further
provided funds to channel into bilingual programs. As a
consequence of all this interest in bilingual schooling,
most of the "hard" literature in this field has come during
the present decade, and today it is continuing to grow in
volume and excellence of quality as attested to by the
professional journals.

In this chapter selected empirical findings and
recommendations by acknowledged leaders in the field of
bilingual education, and research related to the problem
are reviewed. The studies and discussions in the litera-

ture concerned with bilingual education focus on the following areas: philosophical and sociological background, psychological background, linguistic background, and achievement studies.

Philosophical and Sociological Background

Dorothy D. Duhon, Consultant, Modern Foreign Languages, Colorado Department of Education, has clearly set forth the philosophical and sociological reasons for the national concern in bilingual education:

> Strong forces now at work in our country are bringing about a change from a state of unawareness to a realization of what is at stake in the education of the potentially bilingual child, whatever his native language may be. We can no longer afford to ignore the resources latent in this important individual and his counterparts, nor refuse to acknowledge that among the consequences of continuing oversight are social and economic problems that stem from dropouts or inadequate education. On the other hand, the potential gains of our entire country from a well-educated, well-adjusted group of people, able to function effectively in two languages and cultures, are immeasurable.[7]

A. Bruce Gaarder, Specialist in Foreign Languages, U.S. Office of Education, in his keynote remarks at the Conference on Development of Bilingualism in Children of Varying Linguistic and Cultural Heritages, Austin, Texas, January 31, 1967, emphasized the need for bilingual education in the following manner:

> I cannot but suppose that you are all well versed and highly interested in this matter of giving a better kind of education to children

who are necessarily bilingual. That is our primary interest here. Yet I hope that we will go
one step beyond that from the very first and say
that we are also interested in developing bilingualism which did not exist before and which does
not necessarily have to exist. To make plain my
meaning: in Puerto Rico bilingualism is not necessary at all, it is cultivated. But surely in
Texas it is inevitable. You are seeking it in the
one case, you cannot avoid it in the other.[8]
(Italics mine.)

Elsewhere in his keynote remarks Gaarder points to

a situation in the Philippines where the vernacular of a

region was used for teaching in the early grades. It was

supposed to serve as a bridge to the eventual exclusive

use of English. Whereas other experiments in the Philip-

pines had demonstrated the soundness of the two-language

plan, it had failed in this particular school. The

explanation was simply that the parents of this particular

group were firmly convinced that their language was use-

less and that to study it was a waste of school time.

They contaminated the children with this attitude. The

result was that the normal advantage of learning through

the mother tongue was lost. The children did rather

poorly. In other communities, where the mother tongue was

dignified, effectiveness seemed to be of a high level.

This produced children who were successful in handling

English and other things well, and who ultimately became

professionals and businessmen.[9]

In similar cases, Spanish-speaking bilingual chil-

dren have been forced in many cases either to rebel or to

turn against themselves and deny themselves and their
parents in order to get along peacefully in school. Too
often this has resulted in their inability to manipulate
the Spanish language with any competence, thereby creating
for the American school another problem which requires a
special course of instruction as well as special teachers.

Gaarder's philosophy about the bilingual disadvantaged is quite clear from the context of the following
passage:

> We have the whole tide of events going with us.
> I could list from all over the country people who
> are calling, writing, thinking, and talking about
> doing the same things you are here to do. All
> over the country, people are beginning to ask
> themselves: "How could we possibly have given
> these bilingual kids such a dirty deal all these
> years? How is it possible we have done this?" The
> tide is moving with us. It is no time to be timid
> about these things; everything is on our side.
> People are ready for it. They are ready to admit,
> they are even anxious to proclaim that the other
> group is all right already. For whatever reason,
> the word is going out all over the world, "We will
> help you be human in your way." We could not have
> met at a more propitious time. I am so glad to be
> here and to have had a hand in writing this bible.[10]

U.S. Commissioner of Education Harold Howe II
expresses a more international concern when he points out
that bicultural, bilingual programs for Anglo as well as
Mexican-American children may well be the most important
thing for our country:

> The notion of cultural superiority has seri-
> ously harmed the United States in this century in
> its dealings with other peoples of the world.

Whereas European children grow up with the notion
of cultural diversity, and frequently learn two
or even three foreign languages in the course of
their formal schooling, American schools commonly
isolate our children from cultural exchange.

Partially this separation stems from the size
of our country. As businessman or as tourist,
you can go from one end to the other and never
have to speak anything but English. There has
never been any special reason why our schools
should prepare children to speak another tongue.

In the middle of the century, after nearly
150 years of largely ignoring the rest of the
world, we have lumbered into the family of nations
as an international force. A position of international responsibility was thrust upon us, and
we were ill-prepared to assume it.

In fact, one of the great motivations behind
the present set of federal programs for education
was the lack of Americans who could speak foreign
languages or deal with other peoples in terms of
those other peoples' own cultures. The result was
that we often offended people whom we were trying
to help or befriend.[11]

Senator Yarborough, addressing the joint conventions
of the Modern Language Association and the American Council
on the Teaching of Foreign Languages in New York City,
Saturday, December 28, 1968, expressed himself on the
importance of language understanding and appreciation in
the following manner:

. . . And I think that through your efforts to
understand and improve our knowledge of and ability to use languages you are performing the most
fundamental and important task of civilizing man.

Language is at best a crude and imprecise
tool to reflect and express the infinitely subtle
ramifications of our thoughts. But in our increased understanding of the semantic imprecision
of language lies our conviction to understand:
nations must learn to understand nations; peoples
must learn to understand peoples; and man must
learn to understand his fellow man. It is through

language--perhaps through language alone--that
this understanding can be achieved.[12]

From a democratic standpoint second language learning is a cohesive and integrating force in a nation of
many minority groups. That bilingual education is crucial
for national unity is illustrated by the decision taken by
the First National Seminar on Modern Language Teaching,
held in Ottawa, Canada, in November, 1962, and sponsored
by the Canadian Teachers Federation. Decision-makers took
a stand on national bilingualism as a major aim of Canadian
education. If the goals of the seminar are attained, all
Canadians in the future will learn both French and English
as a part of their formal education and second language
training will begin early in the elementary school. In
the elementary program particular attention will be given
to development of positive attitudes toward language
learning.[13] In 1966 Prime Minister Lester B. Pearson
launched a new move to ensure the survival of Canada as a
united country. This program provided for the expansion
of bilingualism--the use of the country's two official
languages, English and French, in government business.

Herschel T. Manuel, Professor Emeritus of Educational Psychology at the University of Texas at Austin,
has been able to see the relationship between English and
Spanish in its proper perspective. He believes that people

cannot work together without a common language. Obviously,
the people of one or of both groups must learn the language
of the other. This, he points out, is the primary basis
for the emphasis on learning English and Spanish as second
languages in the Southwest and, for that matter, in any
area where the two languages exist in the United States.

> The main burden of learning a second language
> obviously falls on the Spanish-speaking child--
> not because it is imposed by some authority, but
> because of the situation into which events of the
> past have brought us. English is the native
> language of the great majority of our people, the
> predominant language of government, business,
> industry, and news media. English for the Spanish-
> speaking child is a necessity if he is to become a
> full participant in the activities of the community,
> the state, and the nation.
> Although Spanish for the English-speaking child
> is less urgent, his learning Spanish would greatly
> improve communication and understanding among our
> people. Spanish deserves a special priority in
> communities in which there is a considerable pro-
> portion of Spanish-speaking residents. In teaching
> Spanish for its local value, the early years are of
> prime importance both because these years are
> favorable to language learning and because better
> communication improves the relations of children of
> different backgrounds.[14]

Cultural, social, and economic benefits are reaped
by those who learn a second language. This is especially
true in those areas where bilingualism is looked upon
favorably by the ethnic groups involved. In Laredo, Texas,
for example, securing even a position as clerk in a business establishment requires a command of English and
Spanish. It is for this reason that the general objectives
of current bilingual education programs aim for instilling

in the pupils a better understanding of children and adults from minority groups. Quite often, one's livelihood may depend on this understanding.

Foreign language experts agree that there are varying degrees of bilingualism. The proficiency of bilinguals may range on a continuum from several hundred words to complete mastery of two languages. Pauline Rojas has clearly stated the degree of bilingualism as it applies to children in this country:

> The overall objective in the education of the
> bilingual child is his integration into the main-
> stream of American life. This does not mean that
> the bilingual child must give up his own language
> and culture, but rather that he must be so educated
> that he will be able to operate in English when
> the situation demands English, and operate in his
> own language when the situation demands the use of
> his own language. It is the obligation of the
> school to make him literate in both languages.
> For the bilingual child to be able to operate
> effectively in the English-speaking world, he must
> acquire the language to the degree necessary for
> whatever role his abilities enable him to play.
> In addition, the school must give him a workable
> knowledge of the behavior patterns and value system
> of the dominant group.[15]

No longer are people who speak a minority language willing to give up their mother tongues as the price of citizenship in this country. Donald D. Walsh points out that:

> There is increasing unwillingness everywhere,
> among peoples who speak a minority language, to
> give up their mother tongues and the ways of life
> that these tongues convey, as the price of first-
> class citizenship in the lands of their birth or

their adoption. And there are heartening signs
of, and results of this unwillingness throughout
the world. . . . In our own country, in Alaska,
over a fifth of the people were until recently
first-class people in Eskimo and Aleut. Now,
with the Alaskan state government and schools
conducted entirely in English, Eskimos and Aleuts
descend inevitably to second-class status--and
they resent the change. The Puerto Ricans in New
York and elsewhere in continental United States
are increasingly bitter because education here
gives no role to Spanish in their lives. The
Mexican-Americans in the Southwest are close to
militancy on this subject, and among American
Indians, new and vigorous voices are raised in
protest.
It is against this background of growing concern and support for the "other language" that I
am speaking. My own concern and support are for
those other languages--apart from English--spoken
as mother tongues in the United States and for
their close relationship to our own foreign-
language teaching. My concern is for bilingualism
and bilingual schooling. . . .[16]

The Spanish-speaking populace is too large to
ignore. The entire Southwest, California, and several
large cities like Miami, New York City, and Chicago contain concentrations of these Spanish-speaking ethnic
groups. Spanish is important not only here in the United
States but also in Mexico, Central and South America, and
Spain. William G. Carr has said:

. . . Over the years I have had close association
with the teacher organizations of Central and
South America, and, I might add for that matter,
of the entire world. I know the leaders of these
organizations pretty well, as well as many individual teachers and officials in their ministries
of education. In the light of this knowledge I
can say that we have in our Spanish-speaking
populations a highly valuable asset which is now
largely wasted. . . .

New opportunity for Latin-Americans in the
North American society can have great impact on
attitudes towards the United States in Central
and South America.[17]

Psychological Background

Factors beyond those that are philosophical and

sociological need to be examined here. There is no ques-

tion that many of our Spanish-speaking bilinguals,

especially Mexican-Americans and Puerto Ricans, often have

the very real problem of trying to decide what they are

and where they actually belong. While these bilinguals

may disdain being called a Mexican or a Puerto Rican, they

do not want to disassociate themselves from their ethnic

group. They are proud of their American birth or citizen-

ship, yet they often seem uncertain how to cash in on

their birthright. Under these conditions one can see why

their self-image cannot be conducive to full participation

in our American society. Consequently, active participa-

tion in the one social institution that could help them

the most, the school, becomes almost impossible, if not

ineffective. Perhaps this is reflected in the low attend-

ance at interschool conferences or meetings. There is no

single national organization of Latin Americans in the

United States at the present time, whether in the area of

religion, education, or politics.

Gaarder sees the use of the mother tongue as one of

the languages of instruction for bilingual children. The

use of the mother tongue is a vehicle for improving the

self-image for the following reasons:

for adding the mother tongue as a teaching medium
    a. to avoid or lessen scholastic retarda-
        tion in children whose mother tongue
        is not the principal school language
    b. to strengthen the bonds between home
        and school
    c. to avoid the alienation from family
        and linguistic community that is com-
        monly the price of rejection of one's
        mother tongue and of complete assimila-
        tion into the dominant linguistic group
    d. to develop strong literacy in the
        mother tongue in order to make it a
        strong asset in the adult's life
for adding a second tongue as a teaching medium
    a. to engage the child's capacity for
        natural, unconscious language learn-
        ing (Anderson, 1960; Penfield 1956;
        and Stern, 1963, Chapter 11)
    b. to avoid the problem of method, apti-
        tude, etc., which beset the usual
        teaching of second languages
    c. to make the second language a means to
        an end rather than an end in itself
        (Stern, Chapter 9)
    d. to increase second language experience
        without crowding the curriculum
    e. plus other well-known reasons which do
        not concern us here: to teach the
        national language, to provide a lingua
        franca or a world status language, for
        cultural enrichment, and economic gain.[18]

Fishman is aware of these psychological implications

when he describes the role of the language teacher in a

setting such as the one mentioned by Gaarder.

    The language teacher, particularly one who is
teaching a language that is utilized in a bilingual setting in which classical and colloquial
variants of the same language exist side by side,

must ask himself: <u>About</u> what topics and to what
range of social types do I want my pupils to be
able to communicate? Only after a decision has
been reached with respect to this question can
greater degrees for bilingualism be pursued in a
realistic manner.[19]

The findings of research pertaining to many aspects

of bilingualism, including the relationship between intel-

ligence and language learning, were reviewed by outstanding

scholars in the field at a conference in Wales. Briefly,

Lewis believes that the development of language inevitably

influences what the child will become. This development,

he maintains, is dependent on (1) the child's physical

well-being and normal growth and development of the nervous

system and of the brain, (2) society's influence on the

child's mental development through language, and (3) a

psychological factor.

Differences in languages and different levels
of language ability create differing patterns of
social behavior and of personal development. Language in very clear terms structures our way of
thinking and behaving.[20]

In recent years language specialists have come to

agree that if language mastery is to take place, it must

begin early in life under the most favorable circumstances.

The Modern Language Association has taken an official

stand on the subject by recommending ten years by grade

twelve as the most ideal number of years of study of a

foreign language.| Walsh has found even this early start
(by grade three) to be too late:

> Mastering a language takes a long, long time,
> and if it is to be accomplished by the end of
> high school, the learning must begin early. . . .
> Even if the early elementary grades were the worst
> time to begin to study a second language, we would
> have to insist that the job takes so long that it
> needs to be started by grade three at the latest.[21]

The neurosurgeon Wilder Penfield of Canada argued
that the brain of a child is plastic, with an unusual
capacity for learning language, but this capacity unfortunately decreases with the passage of years. Penfield
insisted that if second language learning is to be added
to the public school curriculum, the incorporation must be
made according to the changing attitudes of the human
brain and instruction begun when the children are between
the ages of _four_ and _ten_.[22]

Andersson believes that one of the promising
features of bilingual schooling is the early start it
makes in language learning. According to him, the regular
school pattern has already been established and the addition of a second language must seem like something extra-
neous when a child is first introduced to the FLES program
in the third grade. Thus, since most bilingual programs
begin in either pre-first or first grade, this seems most
normal to the child beginning formalized languages instruction. Andersson further states:

> The early start is not only more natural but

also more effective since it takes advantage of
the young child's language-learning ability.
There is a certain inconsistency in the position
taken by many FLES proponents who cite the advantage of early language learning only to waste the
first two or three years, the most favorable
learning period. In contrast, advocates of bilingual teaching regret that they have to wait
until kindergarten or grade one. They look for-
ward to the time when public schools will admit
children of five, four, three, or even two years
of age, for they realize that these earliest
years are the most precious of all for learning
--provided always that we have teachers capable
of understanding the child and of guiding his
learning.[23]

The psychologist John B. Carroll points out that
in spite of advances in theories and practices of teaching
and learning second languages, there is still a lack of a
proven theory. According to him, an examination of the
practices of foreign language teachers and the writings of
several theorists suggests that there are today two major
theories of foreign language learning:

. . . One may be called the audiolingual habit
theory; the other, the cognitive code-learning
theory. The audiolingual habit theory, which is
more or less the "official" theory of the reform
movement in foreign language teaching in the
United States, has the following principal ideas:
(1) Since speech is primary and writing is secondary, the habits to be learned must be learned
first of all as auditory-discrimination responses
and speech responses. (2) Habits must be automa-
tized as much as possible so that they can be
called forth without conscious attention. (3) The
automatization of habits occurs chiefly by practice, that is, by repetition. The audiolingual
habit theory has given rise to a great many
practices in language teaching: the language
laboratory, the structural drill, the mimicry-
memorization technique, and so forth. The cognitive

code-learning theory, on the other hand, may be
thought of as a modified, up-to-date grammar-
translation theory. According to this theory,
learning a language is a process of acquiring
conscious control of the phonological, gram-
matical, and lexical patterns of a second
language, largely through study and analysis of
these patterns as a body of knowledge. The
theory attaches more importance to the learner's
understanding of the structure of the foreign
language than to his facility in using that
structure, since it is believed that provided the
student has a proper degree of cognitive control
over the structures of the language, facility
will develop automatically with use of the language in meaningful situations.[24]

As Carroll points out, the audiolingual habit theory

is the "official" theory of the reform movement in foreign

language teaching in the United States. While it is

difficult to arrive at a precise meaning of what the term

"audiolingual habit theory" means, specialists in the area

of foreign language teaching generally agree that this

theory is characterized by at least four features: (1) use

of an adequate, real-life situation model (hence, the term

"audio-lingual"), (2) contrastive analysis of the learner's

language with the structural differences of the second

language, (3) use of language pattern drills, and (4) min-

imal use of the student's native language.

Carroll further believes that neither theory takes

adequate account of an appreciable body of knowledge that

has accumulated in the study of verbal learning. Among the

facts that he presents are the following:

1. The frequency with which an item is practiced

per se is not so crucial as the frequency with
which it is contrasted with other items with
which it may be confused. Thus, the learning
of items in "pattern-practice" drills would be
improved if instead of simple repetition there
were a constant alternation among varied patterns.

2. The more meaningful the material to be
learned, the greater the facility in learning and
retention. The audiolingual habit theory tends
to play down meaningfulness in favor of producing
automaticity.

3. Other things being equal, materials presented visually are more easily learned than
comparable materials presented aurally. Even
though the objective of teaching may be the attain-
ment of mastery over the auditory and spoken
components of language learning, an adequate theory
of language learning should take account of how the
student handles visual counterparts of the auditory
elements he is learning and help to prescribe the
optimal utilization of these counterparts, such as
printed words, phonetic transcriptions, and other
visual-symbol systems.

4. In learning a skill, it is often the case
that conscious attention to its critical features
and understanding of them will facilitate learning.
This principle is largely ignored by the audiolingual habit theory; it is recognized by the
cognitive code-learning theory. It would imply,
for example, that in teaching pronunciation an
explanation of necessary articulatory movements
would be helpful.

5. The more numerous kinds of association
that are made to an item, the better are learning
and retention. Again this principle seems to
dictate against the use of systems of language
teaching that employ mainly one sensory modality,
namely, hearing. A recent experiment performed
at the Defense Language Institute, West Coast
Branch (Army Language School, Monterey, California)
seems to show that dramatic facilitation of language learning occurs when words denoting concrete
objects and physical actions are associated with
actual motor performances involving those objects
and actions. Thus, the student learns the meaning

of the foreign language word for <u>jump</u> by actually
jumping! Language teaching becomes a sort of
physical exercise both for the students and for
the instructor whose actions they imitate.[25]

Carroll then concludes:

The audiolingual habit theory which is so
prevalent in American foreign language teaching
was, perhaps, fifteen years ago in step with the
state of psychological thinking at that time, but
it is no longer abreast of recent developments.
It is ripe for revision, particularly in the direction of joining with it some of the better elements
of the cognitive code-learning theory. I would
venture to predict that if this can be done, then
teaching based on the revised theory will yield a
dramatic change in effectiveness.[26]

While the audiolingual habit theory continues to be

criticized for its shortcomings, it still forms the under-

lying theoretical basis of bilingual education in elemen-

tary schools where the nature of the curriculum and the

age of the child lend themselves naturally to this method.

It is now generally accepted that bilingual students

develop one of two bilingual systems. One is a compound

or fused system, and the other is a coordinate system.

Nelson Brooks explains this difference:

American psychologists have talked of late
about two systems of handling two languages: a
"compound" system and a "coordinate" system. In
the light of the analysis we have made, the coordinate bilingual chooses one path or the other
<u>before</u> he encodes his message. The compound
bilingual (if we can call him a bilingual) first
encodes his message in his mother tongue, then
restates it--<u>tant bien que mal</u>--in the second
language. A limiting factor in the philological
approach to language learning is that the compound
system seems to be quite satisfactory. There is

no need to abandon the language one is used to,
in fact one never leaves home. The comfort and
security of the mother tongue are ever present.
But observe the implications of this in relation
to the cognitive processes we are describing.
The compound bilingual never experiences the
intellectual freedom and satisfaction of expressing his thought directly in the second language.
Not only is he impeded by the formulations of his
mother tongue, he is also denied the privilege of
fully exploiting the idiomatic potential of the
second language. In fact, the compound system
cheats the learner of some of the most valued
rewards he might otherwise receive.[27]

Brooks clearly points to the "coordinate" system
of handling two languages as the better system. This is
certainly the goal of every person who studies a second
language. Thus, children who attend an elementary school
with a bilingual education program would clearly have the
most favorable circumstances for attaining this coordinate
system because of their age and the nature of two-language
instruction.

Linguistic Background

It is obvious that a large proportion of bilinguals,
whether they be Mexican-Americans, Puerto Ricans, or
Cubans, are socially disadvantaged like other groups in
the United States who are not bilinguals. Robert Lado
believes that this disadvantage results in poor performance
not because they are bilinguals, not because they speak
Spanish, not because they have Mexican or other Hispanic
cultural family tradition.[28] As will be pointed out later

in this chapter, research by Wallace E. Lambert and

associates shows that bilinguals who have adequate social

background can perform better than monolinguals.

Robert Lado also believes that rural and slum

schools have failed to compensate for the social disad-

vantage of their pupils and thus their IQ's steadily

decline as they remain in school.

> Studies also show that low reading ability
> goes with low socio-economic background in the
> family. Thus, the bilingual child will have low
> reading performance, with all that this implies
> in study effectiveness, not because he is a bi-
> lingual, but because of his low socio-economic
> background.[29]

If the literature in bilingual education for the

Spanish-speaking child points out one thing, it is that

the linguistic handicap is overpowering. This agreement

is obvious from an inspection of what the experts in the

area have said and continue to say. This fact is borne

out by the conclusion of the Working Committee on Lin-

guistic and Pedagogical Barriers at the El Paso Conference.

Gaarder reports:

> We prefer to begin the discussion by stating
> our conclusion: unquestionably, in the view of
> these writers, the single greatest linguistic
> barrier to achievement is the lack of strong,
> school-based, community-wide educational programs
> leading to vigorous, curriculum-wide literacy and
> general competence in the Spanish language. The
> lack of such programs is in turn fundamental to
> the removal of an even greater barrier: the
> Spanish-speaking children's relatively low self-
> concept, and the concomitant low expectation as

to their learning capacity held by the children
themselves, their parents, and by the teachers
and administrators in charge of their education.
The view espoused here is that, all things considered, vigorous, curriculum-wide literacy and
general competency in Spanish is the key, the
sine qua non to raising that level of expecta-
tion--even establishing a high level of demand.
Furthermore, of all the barriers to scholastic
achievement, this is the one for which the
schools have been responsible and which the
schools alone can remove.[30]

|The linguistic barrier is so overpowering that it

cannot be fully comprehended unless one main point is made

here. A child, regardless of which ethnic group he belongs

to, is able to conceptualize only to the degree that he

commands his mother tongue. New concepts must be intro-

duced first in the language which he can better use and in

which conceptualization is the easier. Failure to permit

him to use his mother tongue in learning new concepts first

will result in retardation.| John M. Sharp focuses on this

point with extreme clearness:

Unfortunately, the bilingual child of Latin
American background is burdened by serious handicaps that lessen the effectiveness of his education
and, hence, the contribution that he can make to
the total culture of the United States. In the
first place, he is more often than not far from
being a bilingual at the time he enters first grade.
In many cases, his parents speak little or no English, and his first real contact with the English
language occurs when he begins school. English is
no less a foreign language to him than it would be
to a child from Argentina or Colombia! He suddenly finds himself not only with the pressing need
to master an (to him) alien tongue, but, also at
the same time, to make immediate use of it in order
to function as a pupil! His parents, to whom he has

always looked for protection and aid, can be of no
help at all to him in his perplexity. Moreover,
as a result of cultural and economic differences
between the English-speaking and Spanish-speaking
segments of the community, many of the objects,
social relationships and cultural attitudes presented to him in his lessons, though perfectly
familiar to an Anglo youngster, lie without the
Latin American's home experience. Accordingly,
the problem of learning English is, for him,
enormously increased by his unfamiliarity with
what objects and situations the no less unfamiliar
words and phrases stand for.[31]

What Sharp is saying is that the Latin American

child cannot possibly comprehend an idea if it does not

exist in his native culture, which is often the case.

Even more tragic is the fact that so many of these children

do not even handle with any degree of proficiency their so-

called mother tongue:

The Latin American child's peer group is, if
anything, even less helpful to him in his language
problem than is his home. |Forbidden to speak
Spanish at school, he, of course, with relief
returns to his home tongue once he has been re-
leased from his teacher's confining discipline.|
He speaks Spanish with his playmates. But it is
an impoverished Spanish, a language which has been
culturally "beheaded" by its forced separation
from its own literary heritage. Basic vocabulary,
having to do with the home, everyday objects, common human relationships, etc., is on the whole,
fairly "standard Spanish"; but terms designating
objects, customs and relationships introduced by
the dominant English-speaking majority tend to be
loan-words, or, at any rate, non-standard Spanish.
(Interestingly enough, in this situation, the
basic structure of the language, however, has stead-
fastly resisted invasion.)[32]

Sharp further points out that while southwestern

cities are laudably free of enforced segregation on ethnic

minorities, cultural and economic factors do result in considerable de facto segregation. Consequently, large concentrations of Latin Americans, whether Mexican-Americans, Cubans, or Puerto Ricans, naturally spring up in cities of all sizes regardless of geographic location. Thus, many grade schools are attended almost entirely by Spanish-speaking children. Quite often in these schools the use of Spanish is prohibited in the classroom or on the school grounds on the assumption that the children will learn English faster in this manner. English is not taught as a second language in the classroom. Instructional materials are designed primarily for Anglo children and their culture. Sharp pinpoints the problem:

> . . . In these schools--with rare exceptions--the same texts and curricula are in use as in schools in which the majority of pupils are native-speakers of English. The three R's are taught in English from the first grade up, and no classes specifically with English as a foreign language are offered![33]

The solution to these problems according to Sharp are as follows:

1. The fact that English is a foreign language for a large proportion of school children in our Southwest must be frankly recognized, and adequate specialized instruction in English as a foreign language must be built into the elementary school curricula in this part of the United States.

2. Teachers especially trained to conduct programs such as those sketched above should be made available to Southwestern school systems. If necessary, suitable NDEA or M.A. programs

should be instituted for the preparation of such specialists. . . .

    3. Suitable materials for the instruction of our bilinguals should be compiled and published for use in schools. . . .[34]

Studies Related to Achievement

An in-depth study on the relationship of bilingualism to school achievement was carried out at the Ohio State University by Carmen Slominski. This study which reviewed more than twenty-five related articles and projects is summarized by the author this way:

> The present report is a review of some of the investigations which have been done on the subject, and although they differ in point of view as to whether bilingualism alone is a detrimental factor in school learning, I believe that most of them tend to agree that it alone cannot be blamed as the sole factor in some bilinguals' underachievement. It is clear from some of the reports that many bilinguals are ranked as "underachievers" in our schools, after having obtained very low scores on intelligence tests which they obviously could not handle, not because of backwardness and low intelligence as is commonly believed, but merely because the tests were written in a language which to them is foreign. Were these tests adapted to their native language, some of the reports seem to contend, these so-called underachievers might prove to be a great human potential rather than a burden to this country.[35]

Walsh reports a recent study of bilingualism which shows that, as a consequence of the good fit between spoken and written Spanish, when a group of Spanish-speaking Puerto Rican children went through a battery of tests, paired for intelligence and socio-economic background with

a group of English-speaking children, the Spanish-speaking
group scored so much higher that the examiners had to
conclude that the difference was due to the much greater
effectiveness of Spanish as a language for learners.
Because there are so few pronunciations and reading problems for the Spanish-speaking learner, he can make the
transition from learning Spanish to learning in Spanish
months and years before his English-speaking counterpart,
who is still mired down with the bewildering inconsist-
encies of English.[36]

Lambert and his associate, Elizabeth Peal, carried
out a very well-controlled experiment with 164 ten-year-old
Canadian boys and girls. The subjects were divided into
monolinguals in French and bilinguals in French and English. Lambert and Peal arrived at the following conclusions:

> This study found that bilinguals performed
> better than monolinguals on verbal and non-verbal
> intelligence tests. These results were not
> expected because they constitute a clear reversal
> of previously reported findings. . . .
> . . . It is not possible to state from the present
> study whether the more intelligent child became
> bilingual or whether bilingualism aided his intel-
> lectual development, but there is no question about
> the fact that he is superior intellectually. In
> contrast, the monolingual child appears to have a
> more unitary structure of intelligence which he
> must use for all types of intellectual tasks.
> Because of superior intelligence, these bilin-
> gual children are also farther ahead in school than
> the monolinguals and they achieve significantly

better than their classmates in English study, as
would be expected, and in school work in general.
Their superior achievement in school seems to be
dependent on verbal facility. . . .[37]

The Lambert-Peal study certainly indicates that

there is much evidence to the effect that, if school

policy and other conditions (here social) are favorable,

bilingual schooling results in superior educational

achievement. In light of the careful research design

used in this project, one must conclude that the results

are strongly convincing.

A recent study at the Coral Way Elementary School

in Miami, Florida, by Mabel Richardson, supports the

findings of the Lambert-Peal study. In this study, Rich-

ardson attempted with good success to evaluate the effec-

tiveness of an experimental bilingual education program.

Two interrelated phases of this program were investigated.

One purpose of the study was to compare the relative

performance, in the language arts and in arithmetic, of

native English- and Spanish-speaking pupils in an experi-

mental bilingual program with the performance of native

English- and Spanish-speaking pupils in a regular school

program. A second purpose of the study, pertaining only

to pupils in the experimental bilingual program, was to

assess pupil progress in ability to read, understand, and

deal with academic contents in the second language. Two

hypotheses were postulated:

1. There is no significant difference in achieve-
    ment in the language arts and in arithmetic,
    at the same grade levels, between English
    and Spanish-speaking pupils in the experimental
    bilingual groups and English and Spanish-
    speaking pupils in the control groups.

2. There is no significant difference in the
    native and second language proficiency for the
    subjects in the experimental bilingual pro-
    gram as measured by the cooperative Inter-
    American Reading Tests.[38]

After three years of careful testing and recording

of pertinent data, Richardson was able to show that

hypothesis 1 could be accepted, but that hypothesis 2

had to be rejected, even though all groups in the bilingual

program made progressive gains in the second language

during the time of the experiment. Richardson concluded

that:

Within the limitations of this study, the following conclusions appear to be valid:

1. The bilingual program of study was relatively as effective for both English and Spanish-
speaking subjects as the regular curriculum in
achieving progress in the language arts and in
arithmetic. In other words the experimental
subjects were not handicapped in academic achievement in English by studying and learning through
a second language for approximately half of each
school day.

It must be noted here, that in addition to
performing as well as the control group in the
regular curriculum, the English-speaking pupils
were learning a second language and the Spanish-
speaking pupils were learning to read and write
their native language.

2. At the end of the third year of the study
the pupils in the bilingual program were not as
proficient in their second language as they were
in their native language. However, both Spanish
and English-speaking pupils had made impressive
gains in learning both English and Spanish.

3. For the Spanish-speaking pupils the development and preservation of their native
language has been a valuable bonus.

4. For the American pupils an additional
benefit was the opportune chance to learn a foreign language under competent native speaking
teachers, an opportunity which few children in
the United States have at such an early age.

5. The experimental bilingual school, Coral
Way, sets a pattern for similar bilingual schools
and also for other programs of bilingual education.

6. The true significance of this study lies
in the fact that English and Spanish-speaking
pupils made normal progress in a regular school
program and made excellent progress toward becom-
ing bilingual.[39]

Summary Review of the Literature

The old argument that bilingualism can, and does,

seriously injure the child's achievement in school is

unfounded as this review of the literature has pointed

out.

The evidence seems to be that the problem of

bilingual children arises, not from the fact of their

speaking two languages, but from educational policy

affecting the two languages, as in Texas, where instruc-

tion in the public schools is limited to the use of

English. Among those factors which have contributed

negatively to the development of bilinguals are those that are sociological, economic, and linguistic in nature. One fact does stand out, however: bilingualism is eagerly sought, world-wide, by all classes of people, for the intellectual and economic advantages it can bring.

The recent interest in bilingual education in the United States can be attributed to strong social forces within the country. American politicians and educators are asking themselves how it is that this Christian and democratic country has so long neglected its disadvantaged ethnic groups. Somehow it is all right for people to share in this "Great Society" without giving up their tongues and the ways of life that these tongues convey, as the price of first-class citizenship.

American educators have finally found in bilingual education an answer to the problems of retardation among the Spanish-speaking children. The home language has been dignified. Children are permitted to speak their mother tongue in school and to receive formalized instruction through both the mother tongue and the second language. The advocates for early, formalized instruction of language (Carroll, Penfield, and others) have stated their cases convincingly. Children do learn first and second languages better at an early age, and an attempt by many schools to have pre-kindergarten instruction is testimony to this fact.

Linguistically, Gaarder and Sharp, among others, have pointed out the relationship between linguistic handicaps and school achievement.

While the literature on achievement is not too abundant, the Lambert-Peal study and the Richardson experiment have presented strong arguments for the superiority of bilinguals over monolinguals when the social and intelligence variables can be controlled.

CHAPTER III

STATUS OF BILINGUAL EDUCATION LEADING TO

THE DEVELOPMENT OF OPERATIONAL

MODELS AND STRATEGIES

In this chapter operational models and strategies
in bilingual education will be examined. Unfortunately,
no major works in these areas exist. The literature at
the present time is small in volume and lacking in quality
--a reflection of a lack of interest in belingual education until this present decade. From the literature
available, however, the theoretical bases and the operational strategies of these programs are set forth.

The following aspects of bilingual education are
examined in some detail: (1) The Bilingual Education Act,
(2) the Bilingual School, (3) Operational Models, and
(4) Operational Strategies.

The Bilingual Education Act of 1967

In December, 1967, Congress passed the Bilingual
Education Act which became Title VII of the Elementary and
Secondary Education Act of 1965. This bill, the first
ever put before Congress to deal with the problem of

bilingual education, was introduced by Senator Ralph W.
Yarborough (D-Tex.). It has given hope to millions of
non-English-speaking children who have been handicapped by
American education policies for many years. The far-
reaching effects of this bill are just now being felt and
will continue to be felt for a number of years in the
future.

The Bilingual Education Act is designed to offer
the nation's two million non-English-speaking elementary
and secondary pupils a better chance to realize their full
educational aspirations by assisting local school districts
in developing new and imaginative systems of bilingual
education, hopefully tailored to meet the needs of Spanish-
speaking grade and high school pupils who live in the
southwestern states, California, the Middle West, and
Florida; French-speaking students in certain areas along
the United States-Canadian border; and other non-English-
speaking children who reside in widely scattered sections
of the country.[40]

As job opportunities, income levels, economic
advancement, and all aspects of personal and family well-
being are closely related to educational achievement and
the ability to communicate effectively with one another,
this new legislation will help solve the serious learning
difficulties encountered by these pupils.[41]

The original appropriations by Congress to put into effect the provisions of this bill were indeed lofty: 15 million dollars in the first year to allow school districts to initiate comprehensive bilingual systems of teaching non-English students; 30 million dollars for the fiscal year of 1969; and 40 million dollars for the fiscal year of 1970. While Congress authorized an expenditure of 15 million dollars for fiscal 1968, no money was appropriated. The 30 million dollars authorized for fiscal 1969 was compromised by the Senate and the House to the present figure of 7.5 million dollars. While these minimal amounts reflect tokenism, the program is, nevertheless, a step in the right direction for bilingual education. Funding beyond this current year will depend on the degree to which members of Congress are influenced by American educators knowledgeable in carrying out bilingual programs with better than average results.[42]

Applicants for funds under Title VII must apply directly to the U.S. Office of Education, but the state educational agency must be notified of the application and be given the opportunity to offer recommendations. Perhaps the national interest in bilingual education is best evidenced by the submission of over 300 proposals for funding to the U.S. Office of Education. The number of proposals that are likely to be approved for funding is

about twenty-five per cent. As more funding becomes
available in the coming years, the number of bilingual
education programs will increase greatly from an estimated
twelve in operation during the 1968-1969 school year in
this country.[43]

The Bilingual Education Act authorizes funds for
helping local school districts in administering a wide
variety of programs such as: original research and demonstration pilot projects; bilingual education programs for
school systems; the teaching of English as a first language
and the language spoken in the home as a second language;
programs designed to instill in non-English-speaking
students a knowledge of and pride in their ancestral
language and cultural heritage; programs to retrain members
of non-English-speaking ethnic or nationality backgrounds
as teachers; and community efforts to establish closer
cooperation between the school and the home.[44]

Perhaps the attention now being given to bilingual
education programs for Mexican-Americans has completely
overshadowed programs for the other two Spanish-speaking
groups, the Cubans and the Puerto Ricans. As already
reported elsewhere in this study, the Cuban refugees in
the Miami, Florida area have created an extremely serious
problem for the public schools. Because the Dade County
Board of Education has decided to meet this educational

challenge head-on, perhaps nowhere else in the United States is there a better coordinated bilingual education program. Many of the current leaders in this field have participated in the launching of this particular program. Among those prominent educators and authorities associated at one time or another with the program are Paul W. Bell, Pauline Rojas, and Ralph Robinett. Presently, Dr. Rosa Inclán and Dr. Herminia Cantero, two extremely talented Cuban teachers, are in charge of the supervision of this program on a full-time basis.

Walsh points out the serious educational problem of the Puerto Rican children in the New York City public schools. There is but one bilingual program in the Bronx. This program serves less than three-tenths of one per cent of the Puerto Rican children. This is indeed tragic when one considers that there are almost a quarter of a million Puerto Rican children in the public schools of this city.[45] In Chicago, where there is also a sizeable percentage of Spanish-speaking children in the public schools, only one bilingual program has been initiated, and this one began during the 1968-1969 school year. Elsewhere in the country, there are programs for the Spanish-speaking that have strong emphasis on teaching English as a second language, but these programs are not offering instruction via two languages in the core curriculum.

An examination of the literature on the subject of bilingual education reveals that numerous experiments are under way in the New York City schools. These experiments include teaching kindergarten and first-grade children to sing songs in Spanish and English; using Spanish and English books and audio-visual materials on Puerto Rican history and culture; and issuing to Spanish-speaking parents report cards which have Spanish translations of the English texts.

The Bilingual School

A perusal of the literature on bilingualism reveals that there is almost no information on the organization of the bilingual school. Also, it generally omits considera-tion of the process of teaching and learning; the inter-action of teacher, pupils, methods, and materials; and the theories of language and language learning which underlie these happenings. This chapter gives central importance to what happens in the classroom, and it is largely based on such body of theory. The nature and effectiveness of bilingual schooling can neither be assessed nor assured without full consideration of how the school is organized and what practices transpire in the classroom.[46]

What is a bilingual school? A. Bruce Gaarder has pointed this out quite clearly (see page 5). In addition to Gaarder's clear stand on what a bilingual school is,

Mildred Boyer has further defined the term "bilingual program" as applied in real situations. According to her, there are within our borders many programs that are called bilingual and that the labels are often misleading. She calls attention to the fact that "most so-called bilingual programs are programs _for_ bilinguals; the _children_ in them are bilingual, not the programs themselves."[47] This ambiguity of the term, however, is cleared up in the Guidelines for the Bilingual Education Act:

> Bilingual education is instruction in two languages and the use of those two languages as mediums of instruction for any part of or all of the school curriculum. Study of the history and culture associated with a student's mother tongue is considered an integral part of bilingual education.[48]

The Bilingual Education Act is clear in designating for whom bilingual education is intended: American children ages 3-18 whose home language is not English. Any non-English language natively spoken in the United States is eligible, and the local choice should reflect the linguistic make-up of the community making the request for funding through the submission of a formal proposal. As this applies to the Spanish-speaking children, schools in those areas where these children live are expected to propose a Spanish-English program. For Franco-Americans, a French-English program would be appropriate. Other ethnic groups would be served by programs that take into

account the vernacular and English. This would include,
of course, American Indians. More than twenty million
Americans who speak something other than English at home
could benefit from these programs.

So far, bilingual education has been defined. Also,
the people for whom it is intended has been clarified. Now
an attempt will be made to further clarify the meaning of
bilingual education as ground work for the operational
models and strategies that are to follow. American
educators must first determine policy regarding the bilingual program. The choice appears to be clearcut as there
are really only two main categories from which to choose.
One category favors transitional bilingualism, and the
other supports permanent bilingualism.

In transitional bilingualism one or more native
languages are used in the elementary schools as a bridge
into a more prestigious and international language such as
French or English. This has been the case in under-
developed new countries where the local dialects are
inadequate for carrying out communication with the more
civilized countries.

The policy of transitional bilingualism has been
prevalent in the schools of the United States for a long
time. Due to the conviction that being educated in Spanish
is worthless or of little value, Spanish-speaking children

have been denied a chance to be educated in Spanish as well
as in English. Of course, lack of materials has been
partly to blame for this situation, but not entirely so.
The strong anti-German and anti-Japanese feelings during
both world wars resulted in a setback in the education of
bilingual people.[49] This, coupled with a lack of desire
by American people to master foreign languages, increased
our intolerance for anything except English as the language
of instruction in our schools.

The great civil rights movement of the last fifteen
years, however, has made us aware that we are now heading
toward a greater tolerance for minority groups. This has
caused some educators to believe that an integrated society
lies in the near future. Gaarder explains:

> . . . there is underway a terrifying movement
> toward the homogenization of all peoples. . . .
> At the same time, there is an equally strong move-
> ment toward what I call worldwide egalitarianism.
> This double tendency toward equalizing us all has
> two strange and antithetical or complementary
> manifestations. One is toward homogenization,
> toward everybody being alike. The other is in
> the opposite direction. Strangely enough, it is
> toward preservation, placation, and assurance
> given to every group that it is all right already,
> that its way of being is uniquely valuable in
> human terms. . . .[50]

Cheavens is quite aware of this when he points out
the danger of neglect and ignorance of a person's first
language:

> In regard for what is sometimes called the
> dignity of human personality, the native language

should be given every consideration, so intimately is language bound up with the life of any people. In education, effectiveness is closely linked with the choice of the language of instruction. Neglect of native languages, or worse still, their suppression has spelled educational failure repeatedly.[51]

Just how feasible bilingual education becomes for the child in the public schools depends on how well American educators can sell the idea to the public. Senator Yarborough has said:

> You know, and I know, that $7.5 million is nothing but tokenism—that even if the full $30 million had been appropriated, it would make only a dent, but a very significant dent, in the problems faced by those more than three million children who are bruised and battered as they confront the language barrier. And so we need to work to get full funding this next year—$45 million—for bilingual education. That takes work; work by me and work by you. Members of Congress who make the decision about money need convincing by experts like you that money needs to be appropriated and expended for bilingual education. For these three million school children, if there is no bilingual education, there is little education of any sort.[52]

The mass media—radio, television, newspapers, etc.—will have to be fully utilized if community support is to be cultivated. The community must be made knowledgeable in what the bilingual school intends to accomplish through its new program of instruction. The bilingual school will be on exhibit in the public eye for as long as it takes to win the confidence and trust of the community which it serves.

Mildred Boyer offers a word of caution to those who

would develop a bilingual proposal. According to her,
there must be definite, clearcut answers to the following
three questions:

1. Can you get the key people to agree on what
   a bilingual program is? Do they all understand
   the three different concepts of (a) a program
   merely _for_ bilinguals (e.g. ESL), (b) a transitional or bridge program, and (c) a _real_ bilingual program?

2. Can you get the school administration's
   unconditional support, including a willingness
   to find the right teachers?

3. Can you count on the entire school to help
   shoulder responsibility? Social scientists,
   math and science experts, English and ESL
   teachers, linguists, evaluators--all these and.
   perhaps more will be essential for real success, for a bilingual program is not simply a
   question of translating into another language.
   Foreign language teachers cannot manage this
   project alone; it is a project that calls for
   participation by everybody on the Staff.[53]

Operational Models

Gaarder points out that bilingual schools of several
and varied purposes are now and have long been in operation worldwide. In view of the national interest in this
type of schooling, he feels that it is necessary to
establish more schools of this type and to seek to set
forth some guidelines for their organizers.[54]

Among the variables to be taken into consideration
when setting up the bilingual school are the following:
(1) the language being added to the existing program of
instruction, (2) the time and treatment given to each of

the languages, and (3) the use of either monolingual or
bilingual teachers. The decisions regarding these three
variables can affect the program either favorably or
unfavorably.[55]

It is important to know which language is being
added to the existing program of instruction: whether it
is the mother tongue or the other tongue. The dynamics
of teaching and learning are different in each case,
especially in kindergarten and the first two grades.
Taking advantage of the child's ability to grasp language
effortlessly is the chief objective here. Thus, the
child's ability to learn the other language naturally
without the aid of extra, especially trained personnel
must be exploited to its fullest potential. The main
reason for adding the mother tongue is to avoid retardation in the child's mental development which is closely
related to language mastery.[56]

Thus, if one of the many indigenous languages in
Latin America were brought into the schools as a medium of
instruction, the mother tongue would be added. However,
the introduction of English would be another tongue. In
the United States the mother tongue is Spanish for Mexican-
Americans, Cubans, and Puerto Ricans; and English is the
second tongue.

School organization will be affected by the time and

treatment given to each of the languages. Too little or too much time to one language at the expense of the other may be more detrimental than no treatment. The language needs of the students must be carefully assessed before deciding on the amount of time and treatment of each language. This decision is a crucial one as this is often the deciding factor between an effective and an ineffective bilingual program.

Still another crucial variable is whether teachers in the program will be used to teach in only one language or in two. School organization will depend on this decision. The use of monolinguals no doubt limits the possibilities of school organization in terms of student grouping and time scheduling. The use of bilinguals is less confining as the bilingual teacher can fit into any type of school organization and teach both languages, if necessary, during the same period.

Bilingual schools may be either one-way or two-way with regard to student enrollment. In a one-way school there is one group learning two languages; in a two-way school there are two groups, each learning in its own and the other's language. The chart (in condensed form) on page 55 illustrates some of the basic features that differentiate bilingual instructional strategies.

One-Way School

One-way school: One group learning in two languages	Mother tongue added	Equal time and treatment	(No example known)
		Unequal time and treatment	Welsh in Wales, in some schools.
	Second tongue added	Equal time and treatment	In some Welsh-English schools, one language alone on alternate days.
		Unequal time and treatment	Irish in southern Ireland; most bilingual schools in Latin America; English in Wales in some schools; French or Spanish in grade 12 in nine Virginia high schools.

Two-Way School

Two-way school: Two groups, each learning in its own and the other's language	Segregated classes	Equal time and treatment	Spanish-English, Miami, Florida (mixed classes in grades 4-6).
		Unequal time and treatment	(No example known)
	Mixed classes	Unequal time and treatment	Spanish-English, Laredo, Texas; German-American Community School, Berlin-Dahlem.
		Equal time and treatment	English-French, Ecole Active Bilingue-Ecole Internationale de Paris; L'Ecole Internationale SHAPE, St. Germain; the European School, Luxembourg.[57]

Not long ago, concerned educators in bilingual
education from Latin America and the United States were
assembled in Miami, Florida, to write a handbook intended
to provide information for teachers who will be teaching
in bilingual schools. This handbook is one of the products
of the Bilingual Educational Materials Development Center
of the Southeastern Education Laboratory. This Center is
financed jointly by the Office of Overseas Schools of the
United States Department of State and the Southeastern
Education Laboratory. The primary focus of this Center
has been on the bilingual schools in Latin America and
areas in the southeastern United States impacted with non-
English-speaking youth from Latin America. It is from
Razon de Ser of The Bilingual School: A Handbook for
Teachers that the following models of organization are
taken and adapted.[58]

While the organizational pattern of the curriculum
in the bilingual school will vary from school to school,
some generalizations can be made about these patterns.
The following models are presented to show the time allotments to each of the languages taught in the school for
Spanish- and English-speaking children.[59]

In Model I curriculum instruction is equally divided
between English and Spanish. The school day is divided
into two sessions with instruction in one of the two

languages either in the morning or afternoon. While the
instruction may be given in one language and duplicated in
the other, there is also the possibility of either extending it or introducing new concepts of learning.[60] A school
operating under this plan does not exist in the United
States on the elementary level at the present time, if we
consider the full range of time and treatment of languages
from grades one to six. The Coral Way Elementary School
in Miami, Florida, has this type of arrangement for selected students at the fifth and sixth grades. The first four
grades have more than fifty per cent instruction in the
mother tongue.

MODEL I

Bilingual Instruction Across Time

| Spanish | English | Spanish-Speaking Children |
| English | Spanish | English-Speaking Children |

| Morning | Afternoon |

In Model II instruction may be offered in both languages, with about equal time given to each language within
any time block, either separately or in a blended manner.
If monolingual teachers are used in this plan, team teaching appears to be a requisite.[61] On the other hand,

bilingual teachers can work effectively in this type of
time block arrangement, giving immediate translation when
needed to help students completely comprehend new concepts.
Students do not have to wait until the afternoon session
or the next day for reinforcement if they do not understand the lesson in the second tongue. This type of plan
is in operation in the bilingual programs in the State of
Texas, where bilingual staffing is feasible.

MODEL II

Bilingual Instructional Strategy with Either a
Bilingual Teacher or a Teaching Team with at
Least One Team Member Speaking the
Child's Home Language

| S | E | S | E | S | E | S | E | S | E | S | E | S | E |

MODEL III

Spanish Instruction Decreases as
English Instruction Increases

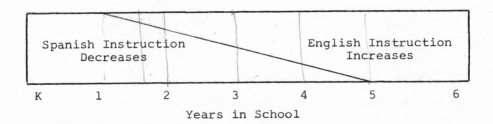

Years in School

In the plan depicted in Model III, instruction begins totally in Spanish and as the student gains mastery of English, Spanish as a language of instruction is phased out, until all instruction is given in English.[62] This type of arrangement would appear to be ideal for Spanish-speaking children except that, if English is the main goal, then bilingualism as such would not be possible as the child's ability to grasp a second language would not be fully exploited and valuable time would be lost.

MODEL IV

English Instruction Decreases as Spanish Instruction Increases

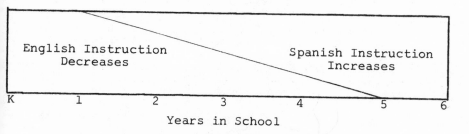

In Model IV, the reverse of Model III, Spanish is the ultimate goal. Instruction in English is diminished gradually and is finally studied as another subject in the curriculum.[63] Such a plan would be functional in a Spanish-speaking country where foreign immigrants and visitors from English-speaking countries have as their

ultimate goal the full command of Spanish. In the United
States this plan would not seem feasible.

MODEL V

Monolingual Instructional Strategy with Language
Differentiated Across Block Times
English Predominant

English
Spanish

In this model the program is offered predominantly
in English, but Spanish is also taught either as another
subject or as the language in which other subjects may be
taught. This is the pattern for many of our Foreign
Languages in Elementary School (FLES) programs in the
United States when Spanish is taught as another language.
If Spanish is used as the language in which other subjects
are taught, we have a bilingual school. Unless it is for
English-speaking children, such a plan is not very effective. This is the plan in operation where there are either
limitations on the use of materials, Spanish or bilingual
teachers, or where the school philosophy gives more
importance to the English language.

MODEL VI

Monolingual Instructional Strategy with Language
Differentiated Across Block Times
Spanish Predominant

Spanish
English

The reverse of Model V is depicted here. Instruction is chiefly in Spanish, but English is also offered,
either as another subject or as the language in which other
subjects are taught.[64] Since English is the official
language in the United States, this plan would not be
longitudinally feasible in our schools. It would, however,
certainly be appropriate at some time during the early
grades in the elementary school. English-speaking people
in Mexico would probably find this model appropriate if
the retention of English were the end goal.

These six models do not exhaust the possibilities
for time and treatment of two-language instruction.
Present bilingual programs in the United States embody
two or three of these plans at separate grade levels and/or
time blocks, but not throughout the entire school program.

Private schools, such as most American schools
abroad or special language schools in this country, can

regulate the admittance of students so that a monolingual
child can only be admitted at the beginning of the program.
The American public school, however, must admit all students regardless of language abilities. The transferring
of students into and within bilingual programs constitutes
a special problem. Monolingual English- or Spanish-
speaking children will be able to function in that part
of the program using their mother tongue, but this is not
so when the second language is used for instruction. So
far the need has been met through orientation and extra
language-skill classes outside the regular curriculum.
Such programs have necessitated the employment of two
special teachers: one for teaching English as a second
language and another for teaching Spanish as a second language.

One thing to keep in mind is that bilingual schooling is not foreign language teaching in the ordinary sense.
It is the ordinary curriculum of any school taught by
fully certified, competent teachers of subject matter, who
are fluent, educated speakers and writers of the other
language. They are not foreign language teachers as such,
but rather foreign language medium teachers.[65] It is for
this reason that, in many cases, unless a teacher is
completely bilingual, she is not expected to teach in other
than her native language. However, bilingual teachers are

a most valuable asset to the bilingual school and may be
used in all models, especially Model II. The areas of
competency needed by teachers in bilingual programs need
not be mentioned here as these areas are covered in
Chapter V under Recommendations and in Appendix B, Teacher
Education.

Operational Strategies

Up to this point the rationale for the bilingual
school has been established. Operational models have been
described, along with possible variations found here in
the United States. The three variables most important to
the bilingual program have been presented and discussed.
All of this is basically theory. The next point to be
clarified is that of operational strategies; that is, what
tools are available to the organizer of the bilingual
school? What operational strategies constitute the bases
of instruction?

The model of operation

An assessment of the language needs of the student
body determines the model selected for organizing the
bilingual school. School policy will determine programs
for students who are bilingual. A different organizational
plan will be required for those who do not speak English,
and another for those who do not speak Spanish. It is

possible that there may be non-Spanish-speaking Latin
American children who for one reason or another have lived
in situations where they learned English first and cannot
function in Spanish at all. Two or three models of operation may have to be used to account for individual differences. (Grouping by language proficiency takes precedence
over intelligence grouping./

The monolingual staff member

Two sets of monolinguals can very well constitute
the staff of a bilingual school if they represent the
Spanish and English languages. More often than not,
staffing is determined by the availability of personnel
rather than by adherence to theoretical considerations.
The depth of the monolingual's training in one language
naturally results in his complete mastery of one culture.
He may function effectively in a two-way bilingual situation if his materials and learning experiences are
carefully coordinated with his counterpart in the other
language. This will, of course, require much planning in
advance as one language will constantly reinforce the
other.

(From the student standpoint, children can identify
completely with one language and one culture at a time
under the direction of a person native to that language
and culture. On the other hand, as the monolingual teacher

is not what the child is striving to be--a bilingual--he does not have the insights of contrastive language analysis so essential for helping bilingual children.)

The bilingual staff member

Few persons are able to function equally well in two languages. This does not mean, however, that a teacher cannot be proficient enough to discharge his teaching assignment with effectiveness. The fact that he himself is a bilingual presents the child with the perfect model. The teacher is already what his students are striving to be--a bilingual. Many times, however, the bilingual may be deficient in some aspects of his second language so that it may be necessary for him to raise his level of command to that needed to teach in both languages within the same time block.

The bilingual teacher is able to plan better his learning activities and to allow for any adjustments that may help his children learn. His plans can be flexible, and he can change them without affecting the plans of others, as in a two-way program with two sets of monolinguals. He is able to check constantly to see if his students are comprehending his lesson presentation. An on-the-spot check reduces the anxiety of insecure children who may be totally lost at times in their second language.

Time and treatment of languages

Arriving at a proper balance of time and treatment of the languages in use is a decision that requires much consideration. One language may be emphasized more than the other. When this happens, the effectiveness of the bilingual school is reduced as bilingualism for the students ceases to be within the realm of possibility. Time and treatment of languages will vary from grade to grade and from group to group within the same grade if grouping has been by language proficiency rather than by intelligence.

Selection of adequate materials

No one set of materials has yet been developed for even the traditional English programs in our public schools. A two-language curriculum requires special material, at least in the Spanish component. Each local system must select, first, materials that are the most adequate, adapt some, and develop others. In bringing to the bilingual school materials from other parts of the country or from abroad, care should be given to a consideration of the degree to which these materials fit local needs. Other considerations are those of cultural and linguistic appropriateness.

Segregated classes

A task that must be faced by the school administrator is that of deciding whether to have segregated
monolingual classes or not. The chief advantage of having
them is that instruction can be better controlled because
materials and learning experiences can be more appropriate
to the members of the class. In the event that the ethnic
make-up of a community is predominantly of one group, then
segregated classes cannot be avoided. Under these circumstances one of the main objectives of the bilingual school
--that of providing a bicultural setting for every pupil--
is not possible. When segregated classes are a matter of
school policy for better instructional climate, however,
the cultural exchange component of the bilingual program
can be provided through special instruction in music,
physical education, and playground activities involving
both groups. Of course, schools that are attended mostly
by one Spanish-speaking group will not have even this
opportunity for cultural exchange.

Non-segregated classes

The chief argument for this type of arrangement is
that every child is placed in a true-to-life situation in
which he comes into daily contact with members of another
culture. The price of cultural exchange for the children,
however, may be more than the administrator is willing to

pay, as adapting materials and learning experiences to this situation creates additional problems. In the final analysis, it seems, both segregated and non-segregated classes are determined by local policy which may or may not be based on sound theoretical considerations.

English as a second language

Non-English-speaking children view English as a foreign language and must be taught English as if it were. Regular procedures in teaching English to native speakers of English do not produce the desired results. English must be reinforced at all times, whether it is being taught as a second language or being used as a medium of instruction.

Spanish for the Spanish-speaking

While English is the national language and, hence, the language that is ultimately the more important, Spanish should not be neglected in a bilingual education program. A special approach should be made through a program of Spanish for the Spanish-speaking. The reason for this is that quite often the Spanish-speaking child is illiterate in Spanish and, hence, his command of this language must be improved.

Placement of transfer students

Even the most stable neighborhood schools are subject to the problems of providing an adequate education
for transfer students. The bilingual school is not only
faced with the normal placement procedure but also with
the added dimension of language. For this reason it
becomes necessary to group students in a bilingual program
in at least three groups: those that are monolingual
speakers of English, those that are monolinguals in Spanish, and those that are bilinguals to some degree. Groups
beyond these three are unrealistic and not feasible, though
certainly desirable. Transfer students may be placed in
these groupings at grade level, and they will at least be
able to perform in that part of the curriculum that uses
their mother tongue. In order to provide language proficiency in the second tongue, the bilingual school should
have two specialists, one to teach English as a second
language and another to teach Spanish as a second language.
Transfer students can thus be given the special language
training needed to allow them to perform in two-language
instruction.

Library services

As in other institutions of learning, the library
plays an important role in the bilingual school. The
librarian is entrusted with the responsibility of procuring

as many books in both languages as is possible. To be
realistic, the number of Spanish books should be more than
a handful and certainly at least three for each pupil in
school.

Since the librarian is charged with the responsibility of giving the student body instruction on the use
of the library as well as in instructional materials, it
is highly desirable that this person be a bilingual. The
rationale behind this contention is that such a person
strongly reinforces what the bilingual school is seeking--
extending its program of bilingualism to all phases of
school activity.

Supportive services

In addition to the administrative and instructional
staff, other members of the school team can contribute to
the bilingual development of the child. Counselors,
secretaries, teacher aides, custodians, cooks, and others,
should reflect the ethnic background of the bilingual
child. Quite often this type of person lives in the community and is readily available for appointment to the
school staff.

Training of staff members

A well planned in-service program by the bilingual
school will ensure the utmost cooperation among the staff.

In many cases the school is able to provide this training by utilizing outstanding members of the staff as well as outside experts for speakers and leaders in designing and implementing new learning materials and strategies. (See Appendix B, Teacher Training.)

Articulation in bilingual education

The problem of articulation is just now being faced by a few bilingual programs. Deciding how to extend the bilingual learning experience into the high school is certain to cause some revamping in school planning at the junior high school level. Bilingual graduates from the elementary schools cannot be put into the conventional foreign language classes. This means that some subjects will have to be taught in Spanish for the benefit of those individuals who wish to continue their bilingualism in a high school context. It is reasonable to expect larger enrollments in the study of third languages as a partial solution to the forthcoming problems of articulated bilingual education programs.

Use of radio and television

Radio and television can be used to provide basic presentation and, certainly, enrichment functions in a bilingual curriculum. (See Appendix A, Radio and Television.)

Community involvement

Interest at the community level must be cultivated.
People must be informed about new trends in education.
The white majority must be made to feel that a bilingual
school will not affect negatively the education of the
Anglo child, but that rather it will enrich it culturally
while bringing the minority ethnic group into the mainstream of American education. Social, business, and
religious agencies in the community are often good sup-
porters of bilingual programs.

Good public relations between the bilingual school
and the mass media are essential for proper, favorable
publicity. The administrator really has no choice in
deciding whether or not to put his school in the public
eye for the simple reason that there are only a few of
these programs in the country. Provision must be made for
receiving a constant flow of visitors.

Provision for evaluation

Like any other school, the bilingual school must
maintain accurate records which reflect the achievement
progress of its student body on the basis of information
provided by standardized tests and other special measurement instruments. As there are few appropriate testing
instruments for bilingual children, the selection of a

competent person to take charge of this assignment is very
important. Outside evaluation should be sought, not
avoided.

CHAPTER IV

AN EXAMINATION OF FIVE EXEMPLARY
BILINGUAL EDUCATION PROGRAMS

Bilingual education has become one of the most
controversial issues in our public schools today. One
major cause of such controversy is directly related to
the fact that bilingual programs have only recently become
realities in communities where there are large concentrations of Spanish-speaking children. The number of these
programs is limited to twelve and they are scattered
throughout the country, but principally they are located
in Miami, New York City, Chicago, Texas, and California.
Programs of this type for Cuban children are limited to
one as, outside of the Miami area, there are really no
concentrations of Cubans large enough to merit full-scale
bilingual programs. Only recently have bilingual programs
at the elementary level been established for Puerto Rican
children. New York City and Chicago have one program each.
The reason for this is that the educational problems of
the Puerto Rican children have not been met head-on by
local school administrators. In many cases the Puerto
Rican problem is viewed as one mammoth remedial reading

project that includes a strong component of instruction in
English as a second language.

Since there are only a few bilingual schools for
Puerto Ricans and Cubans, picking a sample for these two
groups posed no problem; the task was made simple by the
mere fact that few programs of this nature do exist. The
Coral Way Elementary School in Miami, Florida, was chosen
because it represents the most recent attempt to deal with
the problems of educating Spanish-speaking children (here
Cuban) through the bilingual education approach. Public
School 25, The Bilingual School, for Puerto Ricans in New
York City, was selected because it was begun on a larger
scale than the program in Chicago. Also, it afforded an
excellent opportunity to see what had been learned by the
organizers from other bilingual programs in the country.

The bilingual programs for Mexican-Americans
examined in this study were selected on the recommendation
of knowledgeable men in the area of bilingual education.
Three prominent scholars agreed that the following three
programs in Texas were the most outstanding and, therefore,
worth examining in depth: The Nye Elementary School,
United Consolidated Independent School District (Laredo);
the Garfield Elementary School, Del Rio Independent School
District; and the J. T. Brackenridge Elementary School,
San Antonio Independent School District.[66] No sampling was

taken from the State of California as it is generally
agreed that Texas bilingual programs are in a more advanced
stage of development at the present time.

The programs represented in this study are considered to be among the best "real" bilingual education
projects in the United States. The intent of this study
was to examine in depth all of these programs and to pick
out the outstanding features which make them successful
in carrying out the basic philosophy and theory of bilingual education for the non-English-speaking Latin American
children in our elementary schools. As all of these
programs are currently operative only at the elementary
level, this study is limited in this respect. However, it
should be pointed out that there are no bilingual education
programs beyond the sixth grade in the school districts
which have these programs. Only one school system has
attempted to articulate its bilingual program into the
junior high school, and the results have been less than
successful. The Anglo children have shied away from the
program, leaving it mostly to the Spanish-speaking ethnic
group. Lack of administrative support, coupled with
staffing problems, has been cited as the chief obstacle
to articulation.

This does not mean that there have not been attempts
to teach core curriculum subjects in a foreign language at

the high school level. Joseph Murphy reports numerous experiments in this field.[67] However, there was one experiment in bilingual instruction on the junior high school level in several schools in New York City. The program's experimental variable consisted of bilingual science instruction and an accelerated course in the Spanish language. This experiment is still continuing, but does not represent an all-out, full commitment in bilingual schooling for the entire school.[68]

The data collected through questionnaires and on-the-spot visitations has been reduced to four general categories and is presented as follows: (1) demographic description, (2) instrument analysis, (3) response, and (4) reports and generalizations. Only the most salient features of each program are presented here. Each program, to be sure, contained some outstanding features not found in the other programs, or contained elements carried out in such a superior manner as to be conspicuous.

Demographic Description

Cubans

Of the three ethnic groups represented in this study, the Cuban has turned out to be the most easily assimilated into the American mainstream. Factors that contribute to this adaptation are the following: (1) The Cuban refugee represents the middle and upper class in

Cuba. For the most part, these refugees come from homes
in which the educational tradition is very strong. Until
the Castro regime began to regulate the migration of professionals, the United States was the recipient of some of
the most talented immigrants to come to our shores.
(2) Another factor that has helped the Cuban to be assimilated into our culture is the fact that most of them have
light complexions. Unless they are Negro, they have not
been subjected to racial discrimination. (3) The strong
nationalistic spirit of the Cuban has enabled him to take
pride in his ethnic background and to be self-reliant in
matters of livelihood. Unemployment among Cubans is relatively low compared to other Spanish-speaking groups.
(4) The special efforts by the U.S. Department of State in
helping to locate entire Cuban families in the United
States have also reduced the possibility of broken family
ties, and subsequent enrollment on the lists of welfare
agencies. Many Cubans have been helped to relocate in
jobs for which they already had marketable skills. (5) The
never-dying spirit of the Cuban Revolution has provided
these people with a dream to return to their homeland in
the near future. Many consider their stay here to be a
temporary one.

During the time that the United States and Cuba were
on good diplomatic relations, the number of Cubans coming

into this country was limited, not so much by immigration quotas, as by a lack of desire on the part of the Cuban people to leave their island. The proximity of Cuba to Miami, however, did provide easy access to those who wished to come to live here.

As in the case of many towns along the Mexican border, Miami has long had a bilingual population. Tourism and commerce with the Latin American countries has kept alive the need for bilingualism and biculturalism. Today, the community continues to have even a greater need for educated bilingual clerks in its stores, bilingual executives in its businesses, bilingual doctors, bilingual secretaries, bilingual lawyers, bilingual policemen, etc. In brief, the bilingual has an advantage in almost every category of employment.

After the first year of the Fidel Castro regime, however, many Cuban families began to pour into the Miami area, thus creating for the public schools special problems of instruction. By 1962 the problem had become so acute that the Dade County Board of Education decided to meet the challenge head-on. How to provide the Spanish-speaking Cuban pupil an appropriate school program became the task at hand. In the spring of 1963, it was decided that one elementary school out of Dade County's 150 would offer a bilingual program. Before launching this special program,

a very careful assessment of educational objectives was
undertaken to incorporate experiences gained from examining its second language and vernacular programs for the
Cuban refugee already attending the traditional school
programs for Anglos in the Dade County schools.

The Coral Way Elementary School in Miami, Florida,
is in a neighborhood broadly representative of all economic
levels, but mostly middle class. At the time that the
bilingual program was initiated in 1963, Cuban children
had to be bussed to the school to raise the number of Cuban
pupils to 30 per cent. Within two or three years, however,
the percentage of Cuban children had risen to an ideal
50 per cent. The latest figures show that there are now
almost 80 per cent Cuban children attending this school.
Nearly all the Cuban children are white except for a small
handful of Negroes, both Cuban and American.

Puerto Ricans

A Puerto Rican community has existed in New York
City for well over one hundred years. The very first
Puerto Ricans came to this country for purposes of trade.
These first immigrants were followed by a considerable
number of political exiles and others fleeing Spanish rule
on the island. As a result of our victory over Spain in
the Spanish-American War, Puerto Rico came under the
administration of the United States. In 1917 Congress

passed the Jones Act, thus making Puerto Ricans official citizens of this country.[69] Migration to the mainland increased rapidly at this time as there was a demand for labor in this country, and Puerto Ricans were desirous of leaving an over-populated island suffering from economic and unemployment problems.

The drain on American manpower during World War II created an acute demand for labor. Consequently, the number of Puerto Ricans coming to the United States reached an all-time high. This migration reached its peak during the 1950's when air travel between Puerto Rico and this country became economically feasible for travel purposes. It is this ease of back and forth travel between island and mainland that has reinforced the bilingual and bi-cultural nature of Puerto Rican life in New York City.[70]

White and Negro Puerto Ricans have had to adjust to new attitudes toward race in the United States. As a result, most of them live in concentrated Puerto Rican neighborhoods in New York City, while only a very few live outside the city or in urban areas of lesser Puerto Rican population concentration.[71] According to the 1960 U.S. Bureau of the Census, there were over 900,000 individuals of Puerto Rican birth living in the United States, with over 600,000 of them in New York City. This information is now almost ten years old and, consequently, not very accurate. A more realistic estimate would be nearly 1,000,000 Puerto Ricans in New York City alone, not counting those who live in other parts of the country.

While generalizations about ethnic groups are difficult to make, it can be said that most of the Puerto Ricans living in the Greater New York area are from the lower working class and live generally in the run-down slums of this metropolis. Although these Spanish-speaking people live amidst plenty, they have not shared the riches of this country. Rather, poverty has been their lot, for the most part.

The anthropologist Oscar Lewis asserts that the Puerto Rican is so helpless because he lives in a society whose highest expression is in terms of material wealth. According to Lewis, the Puerto Rican inherits a "culture of poverty." Even when economic benefits are within his reach, the subculture of poverty persists from generation to generation in a legacy of outlawry and despair. Poverty can be eliminated, but not the "culture of poverty." Lewis cites Cuba as an example where people are poor and still have to live in slums, but the culture of poverty is gone. The poor have been incorporated into the mainstream of society; they have been given a sense of participation in history. For them there is a tomorrow.[72]

Public School No. 25, The Bilingual School, in New

York City represents the first all-out experiment in bilingual education for Puerto Rican children at the elementary level. The neighborhood is in the Bronx, in an extremely low socio-economic environment. The school enrollment is approximately 800, 87 per cent of which is Puerto Rican, with the other 13 per cent mostly Negro. The bilingual program started in the fall of 1968, in an old school building that was vacated for this purpose. Bilingual instruction was offered simultaneously at all six grade levels, in marked contrast to other bilingual programs that have introduced this type of instruction gradually, grade by grade.

Mexican-Americans

The first white people to migrate into what is now the American Southwest were Spanish-speaking and came by way of Mexico during the period of Spain's colonial expansion and settled in portions of the Southwest in the first decades of the Seventeenth Century. After its Independence in 1820, Mexico encouraged the migration of English-speaking Americans into the Southwest as few Mexican colonists were moving there. The response was more than the Mexican government had expected and, consequently, it attempted to regulate this immigration. International trouble developed over this problem and resulted in the

Mexican War in which Mexico lost all of its territory
north of the Rio Grande River.

Mexicans living in the Southwest did not return to
Mexico. They preferred to remain in the land of their
birth--a land that had belonged to them for generations.
They were Americans with a language and culture different
from the language and culture of the dominant group today.
Post-war resentment did not abate easily for many years
after the Mexican War.

Whereas other ethnic groups in the United States
have been assimilated into the American mainstream, this
is not true of the Mexican-American. He has not been
willing to abandon his cultural and linguistic heritage as
the price for belonging to the dominant culture. The
Mexican-American has not possessed the strong materialistic
drive of the Anglo-American. Perhaps this can be explained
by the fact that so many immigrants from Mexico were at low
levels on the economic scale when they came to this country. They were unskilled and semi-skilled laborers who
hoped for better opportunities for themselves and their
heirs. Both the Mexican who remained in the Southwest
after the Mexican War and the one who fled the Mexican
Social Revolution of 1910 bequeathed to their children a
legacy of poverty. And as is the usual case, poverty is
accompanied by a lack of education.

Today, Mexican-Americans are found in all walks of life but relatively few are in positions that require advanced formal education. Most are manual laborers or semi-skilled workers. Rodriquez from the Mexican-American Affairs Unit in the U.S. Office of Education estimates that there are less than two hundred Ph.D.'s among our five million Mexican-American citizens.[73]

In addition to the large number of Mexican-Americans living in the Southwest and California, there are thousands in different parts of the Middle West and most large cities. New York City, Chicago, and Detroit, for example, contain sizeable Mexican-American communities.

Perhaps the most tragic factor reflecting on the plight of the Mexican-American is his educational shortcomings. According to the NEA-Tucson Survey of 1966:

> The most acute educational problem in the Southwest is that which involves Mexican-American children. In the elementary and secondary schools of five states in that region--Arizona, California, Colorado, New Mexico, and Texas--there are approximately 1.75 million children with Spanish surnames. Many of these young people experience academic failure in school. At best, they have limited success. A large percentage become school dropouts.[74]

To the United Consolidated School District of Webb County in Laredo, Texas, goes the honor of the second most recent bilingual education program in the United States. Three elementary schools are presently participating in the bilingual program. Of these three, the largest, Nye

Elementary School, was chosen for examination in this study. This school is located in one of the most bilingual cities along the Texas-Mexico border. While the school is located in a nice residential neighborhood, it draws students from many socio-economic backgrounds. At the present time the school enrollment is 519, with 40 per cent Anglos and 60 per cent Mexican-Americans. The location of an Air Force base in its vicinity adds to the school population, thus differentiating further the ethnic composition of the school.

Del Rio is a town of 25,000 on the north side of the Rio Grande River in Texas. It is a bilingual-bicultural community of about 50 per cent Anglos and 50 per cent Mexican-Americans. The town is served by schools of two independent districts and some parochial schools. Many pupils do not speak English until entering school. Close proximity to Mexico provides strong ethnic and language identification for the children in the public schools.

The bilingual education experiment in the Del Rio school system started in the fall of 1966, with four of the eight first-grade classes at the Garfield Elementary School participating. At the beginning of the next year, as the first group advanced to the second grade, the bilingual program was expanded to two levels. This year

there are three grades. Although the school has an
enrollment of approximately 750 pupils, only 370 are
involved in the bilingual program. Of these, 85 per cent
are Mexican-Americans and the other 15 per cent are Anglos,
with very few Negroes included.

Next to the Miami programs, the San Antonio Independent School District has the biggest bilingual program
in the country. Some 4,000 Mexican-American students in
nine elementary schools are involved in a bilingual language development program conducted in cooperation with
the Southwest Educational Development Laboratory.[75] Of
the nine elementary schools involved in this ambitious
project, the J. T. Brackenridge Elementary School was
chosen for an in-depth examination. All of the school's
1,250 pupils are Mexican-Americans with the exception of
10 Anglo and Negro students. The school is located in a
very low socio-economic neighborhood. The problems of
these youngsters are typical of other Mexican-American
children living in the Southwest: language barrier, dire
poverty, broken homes, etc. About 65 per cent of the
children are on welfare status. The bilingual program is
limited to less than 50 per cent of the school enrollment
since less than half of the teachers are bilingual.

Instrument Analysis

As previously pointed out in Chapter II, the literature on the nature of bilingual programs does not deal with the basics of program administration. Most of the articles deal exclusively with the philosophical, psychological, and linguistic problems. The problems that naturally arise in scheduling, placement, articulation, etc., are only briefly mentioned. Thus, one of the objectives in this study was to develop an instrument that would show the administrative organization of bilingual programs. Briefly, the following aspects are taken into account by the instrument: administrative support, kind of community, type of school, statement of objectives, time and treatment of languages, placement procedures, articulation, teaching strategies, radio and television, extra-curricular activities, acculturation, staffing, teacher training, community involvement, materials, library use, evaluation procedures, and comments and conclusions. (See Chapter III for an explanation of these terms.)

Response

Today bilingual education is one of the current innovations in our public schools. Those schools with excellent programs, such as the one visited by the writer, are accustomed to receiving visitors from all parts of the country and, indeed, from out of the country. Conse-

quently, the administrative officers in charge of these

programs are quite willing to exhibit their innovative

projects. The immediate directors of these programs point

out that visitors are their best publicity agents as these

individuals are usually interested educators in positions

of prestige and influence in institutions of higher learn-

ing. Only in one of the five schools visited, did the

writer feel that not all informational resources were made

available to him on a "see-it-as-it-is" basis. In spite

of the small number of these programs in the United States,

it appears that no one person has taken the time to visit

all of them, as concerned supervisors frequently sought

the advice of the writer on various aspects of bilingual

education. Copies of this study have been requested by

several of these educators.

Reports and Generalizations

Data made available through the use of the instru-

ment is here presented to point out the most outstanding

features of the five bilingual programs that comprise this

study. An attempt is made to keep generalizations as brief

as possible.

Administrative support

The amount of personal concern shown by administra-

tive officers in all the bilingual programs visited was

outstanding in terms of support and cooperation. In one
instance the superintendent was more knowledgeable in the
theoretical and practical aspects of bilingual education
than were his staff members, including the supervisor.
This high-echelon administrative officer is considered a
national leader in the bilingual schooling movement and is
constantly involved in leadership roles, locally and state-
wide, in Texas. The other administrative officers are
enthusiastic advocates of bilingual schooling and have
taken the trouble to at least learn something about the
language of the Spanish-speaking minority group.

These individuals have taken a strong public stand
on the merits of bilingual education and accept the extra
headaches that go with the administration of these programs. To them has fallen the task of winning community
support which, in some cases, has meant putting their
professional reputations on the line.

Type of bilingual program

The three types of bilingual programs have been
identified and discussed in Chapter II. While the schools
visited all have bilingual programs, there is a marked
difference in the degree of time and treatment given to
the two languages of instruction, English and Spanish.
For example, the program at the Coral Way Elementary School
is, unquestionably, a real bilingual situation. Instruc-

tion is given in English and Spanish from the first grade through the sixth grade. Time allotments to the second language are increased along each grade level, until they are equal to those given to the mother tongue by the fifth or sixth grades.

The Nye Elementary School is especially bilingual at the first and second grades. At the third-grade level Spanish as a medium of instruction is used approximately one-third of the time as compared to two-thirds time for English. At grades four, five, and six, one hour of the Spanish language is offered every day. This instruction may or may not be in the area of the curriculum. The choice is left to the discretion of the teacher. In addition, there are two extra hours per week of Spanish instruction in the areas of arithmetic, social studies, or science. The language arts component is conducted entirely in English. It would appear that the program is more oriented toward English than toward Spanish as there is no evidence of a 50-50 ratio in time and treatment given to the two languages of instruction in the upper grades.

The Garfield Elementary School has a strong emphasis on both languages as mediums of instruction. An examination of the program reveals that there exists two-language instruction only at the first four grades. The curriculum is broken down into the language arts component (reading, writing, spelling, and phonics), social studies, physical education, music, art, and library use. The amount of time given to the two languages is flexible, and the teacher has the privilege of always using the language that will best assure meaningful comprehension at any time necessary.

The J. T. Brackenridge Elementary School has a more restricted curriculum than any of the other programs examined in this study. The curriculum for the Language-Bilingual Education Program is written by curriculum and language specialists, pilot tested in the classrooms, then refined and revised as a result of the experiences of the teacher and the pupils. Bilingual materials under development and being pilot tested in this school include: Oral Language--Science, grades 1 through 5; Social Studies, grades 1 through 3; Self-Concept, grade 1; Mathematics, grade 1; Reading, grade 1; and Composition, grade 1. From the materials used we see that the time and treatment given the two languages of instruction are definitely substantial although far from a 50-50 ratio by the time the child reaches the sixth grade. There is a bilingual program whenever there is a bilingual teacher. Otherwise, a large portion of the student body is excluded from actual participation in the program.

Public School No. 25, The Bilingual School, in New

York City, is an experimental project in which both English
and Spanish are used as languages of instruction. Thus,
in many cases, children are being taught subjects such as
mathematics, science, and social studies in Spanish. The
central objective of the program is to develop bilingual
proficiency in reading, writing, understanding, and speaking. This program differs from the other four in that it
began as an all-out effort in bilingual education. In the
fall of 1968, programs were started at all six grade
levels.

Statement of objectives

Without exception, the objectives of each program
are spelled out in clear, precise terms. The reason for
this is that most of the funding agencies require that
these objectives be so stated. An examination of the
several statements of objectives reveals that three fundamental objectives incorporate the essence of the strategic
base of the bilingual approach to cross-ethnic education.

The first objective is to improve the self-image of
the Spanish-speaking child through a carefully structured
program of the basic skills of listening, speaking, reading, and writing in his own native language so that he may
express himself in standard Spanish and learn about the
culture from which he comes.

The second major objective is to enable the Spanish-

speaking child to move more easily from his mother tongue
and culture to that of the dominant Anglo-American social
structure. This is to facilitate his intellectual and
conceptual development in English so that he can compete
on an equal basis with his Anglo peers.

The third objective is to provide the Anglo an
opportunity to improve his ability to function effectively
in a second language and a second culture. The imple-
mentation of objectives one and thrée combine, theoretically, to create a receptive, functionally penetrable
environment for both Mexican- and Anglo-Americans.

Placement procedures

The placement of students in the best possible
learning situation still remains a problem to administrators concerned with bilingual schooling. Part of the
problem is the lack of reliable instruments to determine
a Spanish-speaking child's level of intelligence and
achievement. Another obstacle is that of determining the
degree of bilingualism that a student may or may not have.
The solution to this problem of student placement, however,
appears to be handled in the following manner: All students are divided into three groups; one group consists of
monolingual Spanish-speaking children, another group is
made up of monolingual English-speaking children, and
another group is composed of bilinguals. Grouping of

students by language proficiency takes precedence over grouping by intelligence or other factors.

One of the best solutions to bilingual placement was that of the Del Rio Garfield Elementary School. In grade one, for example, eight sections are divided in the following manner: two sections of monolingual Spanish-speakers, two sections of bilinguals, and four sections of "regular" students--those whose language skills were somewhere between monolingual and bilingual. Thus a student, regardless of his level of bilingualism, may be assigned to the group in which he can best achieve. In programs like Nye Elementary School and J. T. Brackenridge Elementary School, however, the number of sections do not present a problem as the whole student body is linguistically homogeneous.

Articulation

Only the Coral Way Elementary School has had to face the problem of articulation beyond the grade school. In the junior high school where bilingual education has been tried, the results have been less than satisfactory. Providing tracks for bilingual education continuation is educationally sound though not administratively possible at the present time.

Problems of scheduling discourage children to continue beyond the sixth grade. Anglo children usually do

not wish to continue core curriculum courses in the Spanish
language because they are too difficult, or because they
would rather be in a more normal class situation. Spanish
for the Spanish-speaking Cuban students is perhaps an
answer to one ethnic group's desire to pursue authentic
foreign language instruction.

Many educators believe that bilingual education
does not have a place beyond the elementary school. The
writer sees this as a current problem, too, but foresees
the time when it will be solved through a more cooperative
junior high school administration.

Teachers of foreign languages in the high schools
look at the bilingual graduates from the elementary schools
as a source of future delight and alarm. What to do with
the bilingual in the high school foreign language classes
will certainly be a problem in the future. A possible
solution might be to challenge these students to enter a
third language situation. Of course, these students will
finally fulfill the expectations of college teachers of
Spanish who have long hoped for the day when students would
be able to appreciate literature courses without language
difficulty.

To this writer's knowledge, there is only one college that offers a bilingual (English and Spanish) curriculum. It is the College of the Pacific. Here instruction

is given in two languages, and bilingualism, for both
Spanish-speaking and English-speaking students, is a by-
product rather than a predetermined goal.

Instructional strategies

Teachers in bilingual programs are not foreign
language teachers in the usual sense. They are foreign
language medium specialists. They do not teach foreign
language as such, but rather use foreign language as a
medium of instruction. Consequently, the teacher must be
aware of the principles of teaching a second language.
Such a teacher constantly uses one language to reinforce
the other through a teaching strategy based upon the total
school curriculum. New concepts are introduced first in
the mother tongue of the child so that full conceptualization may take place. Such an approach requires careful
lesson planning and instructional materials development by
both sets of monolinguals teaching in a bilingual program.
To produce synergic bilingual learning situations, cooperative interaction in planning between the two is essential.
This problem is somewhat minimized when bilingual teachers
are permitted to teach in both languages.

After initial introduction of new concepts in the
mother tongue, there appear to be two methods of reinforc-
ing them in the second language. One is by presenting the

same material in the second language, and the other is to relate it to other course content.

In those programs where segregated classes were scheduled in order to give special attention to the peculiar problems of either Spanish-speaking or English-speaking children, different approaches were noted. Spanish was taught as a second language to Anglos, but as a first language to Latin Americans. Conversely, English was taught as a second language to Latin Americans, but as a first language to Anglos.

The most innovative strategy was observed at the Coral Way Elementary School where selected fifth and sixth grade pupils are divided on a non-graded basis and team-taught by two sets of monolingual teachers, one set Cuban and the other Anglo. These students, divided into six groups and into two sections, receive two and a half hours of instruction in both languages. Close coordination in planning by both sets of monolingual teachers is made possible by released time for this purpose. In order to cover the entire elementary school program, some subjects are treated in three-week blocks of time. For example, science or mathematics may be taught in block times at three-week intervals. This allows more time for the other subjects without the pressure of time.

Much oral practice is used on a choral and individ-

ual basis to master difficult language structures whether
in English or Spanish. Activity-oriented learning experiences are the rule rather than the exception in working
with these children.

Radio and television

The use of radio and television is by far the most
neglected instructional tool. The five programs visited
did not have available television programming for either
basic presentation or for enrichment. This is particularly
tragic in the Mexican-American bilingual programs where
commercial stations do present a steady stream of good
Spanish programs. Television would certainly be a partial
answer to the present bilingual teacher shortage. In
addition to basic presentation, however, there exist great
possibilities in using commercial programming for enrichment purposes. Appendix A has been included to elaborate
on the possible uses of radio and television in bilingual
programs.

Supportive personnel

Supportive personnel are identified as individuals
other than the administration and the teaching staff. Nye
Elementary School in Laredo was especially strong in this
aspect. Only the school nurse was Anglo, but she was able
to comprehend Spanish and was knowledgeable about the

health problems peculiar to Mexican-American children.
Coral Way Elementary School is also strong in this respect
as it employs several bilinguals for kitchen help, janito-
rial staff, library services, etc.

Nye Elementary teachers receive strong support from
truly bilingual aides. These aides are high school graduates and have an excellent command of both languages.
Many of the reading problems encountered by students are
referred to an aide who can provide good instruction in
this area. The availability of this source of personnel
is limitless in Laredo.

Acculturation

The three programs investigated in Texas for
Mexican-Americans reveal that the degree of bilingualism
was about the same for biculturalism. Laredo shows a
strong ethnic group identification in things Mexican-
American; Del Rio is weaker in this respect; and San
Antonio shows the least amount of acculturation. This is
also true for the value given to the Spanish language.
Mexican, not Spanish, culture is looked upon as the mother
culture. The materials used definitely reflect things
Mexican-American first, and then Mexican. Perhaps the
strongest cultural indoctrination is done through music
and dancing activities in which Mexican folk songs and
dances received equal time.

In Miami, the acculturation process is more sophisticated and complete. The Cuban teachers are extremely
nationalistic and expect the students to behave like
"Cuban" children. Since the materials were developed
especially for this ethnic group, the children are exposed
daily to Cuban culture. The large Cuban population in
Miami is another factor that helps in this regard. Down-
town Miami has a considerable number of Cuban business
establishments. The clerks and employees of these businesses are, for the most part, bilingual and cater to
things Cuban. In addition, a Cuban barrio, complete with
all the necessary services, reinforces Cuban culture after
school hours. Persistent talk about returning to the
Island lends additional support in this regard.

In New York City, Puerto Ricans have been confined,
both by circumstance and choice, to a large barrio where,
as in Miami, there are complete services to be found. The
Puerto Rican is reminded daily of who he is by the circle
of friends with whom he spends most of his after-school
hours. Direct plane flights from New York to Puerto Rico
are within the economic range of many Puerto Ricans. The
news media provide additional reinforcement. Channel 42
televises Spanish programs, many of them catering especially to viewers of Puerto Rican descent. One newspaper,

a daily, is for Puerto Ricans and other Spanish-speaking
clientele.

Staffing

Staffing for the bilingual programs has been a
major problem everywhere. With the exception of Coral Way
Elementary School and Public School Number 25 of New York
City, each school is beset by problems of bilingual
teacher recruitment. At the J. T. Brackenridge School,
the bilingual program is limited to the number of bilingual
teachers on the staff, a number less than half. Only a few
Anglos can be classified as bilinguals. Most of them are
English-speaking monolinguals. The reason for this is
that only a small percentage of Latin Americans can fulfill
the state requirements for certification. Also, when
bilingual programs were initiated in schools where a
permanent staff was already committed, many of the monolinguals did not wish to leave the schools for other
assignments in the system.

The degree of bilingualism attained by Mexican-
American teachers in Laredo is excellent; in Del Rio, it
is fair; and in San Antonio, the bilingual teacher is more
oriented to self-expression in English. In Miami, the
teachers are for the most part monolinguals, though the
Cuban teachers have more of an edge in two-language facility.

Teacher training

A concern for the recruitment and retention of good
teachers for bilingual programs is much evidenced by local
in-service training programs at all schools. For the most
part, these programs take place during the summer at the
expense of the local school system. In many cases this
training can be provided through pre-school programs that
have been set up under Head Start. Professional in-service
training for staff members is provided on a weekly basis.
One school, the J. T. Brackenridge Elementary School, makes
use of micro-teaching. It has available the facilities in
a special room where teachers can see instant replays of
their instructional performance. Evaluation comes from
the use of a self-evaluation tool, or from a critique by
the supervisor who makes at least one visit to the school
per week. San Antonio is very much ahead of the rest of
the country in the number and quality of programs designed
especially for training teachers for bilingual programs,
regardless of the teacher's stage of personal development.
Our Lady of the Lake College, for example, sponsors a
week-end commuters' institute for teachers who are unable
to leave San Antonio to attend institutes away from home
for extended periods of time. This particular program
offers instruction in general linguistics, instructional
methodology, Spanish oral proficiency, English as a second

language, etc. In addition, it provides demonstration classes in which a master teacher demonstrates the best instructional strategies for working in a bilingual school situation. Project Teacher Excellence identifies young men and women early in their college careers and assigns them to pre-service internships at bilingual schools which provide opportunities for participation in instructional settings with a bilingual emphasis.

Another source of teacher training is the summer EPDA institute. At the present time only a few colleges and universities offer a program of special training for teachers of bilingual schools. The program offerings reflect a variational planned experience base. (See Appendix B, Teacher Education, for course offerings.)

Community support

Since bilingual education programs continue to be controversial to the average community citizen, a special effort has to be made to attain local support. Fortunately, where there are strong ties, at least linguistically, with a foreign country, as in Miami, Del Rio, Laredo, and San Antonio; or where the attitude of the metropolis is extremely cosmopolitan, as in New York City, the business community is easily sold on the merits of bilingualism. The major reason for such easy sale has an economic base. Businessmen increase profits when the income level of

Americans of Latin descent is increased. Parental involvement, though, has been achieved, to a degree, when general
resistance to these programs has been overcome. Most
parents are happy to see their children participating in a
new and unique learning adventure. In almost all cases,
each bilingual project has become a showplace for the
community, and the news media have covered the story
thoroughly and often. In San Antonio, entire classes are
invited by the local school television station to present
live lessons. In one case, an entire class of Mexican-
American children is being flown to New York to give a
demonstration. The professional journals, too, have
repeatedly carried articles on the merits of these programs. The Senate hearings on bilingualism, conducted by
Senator Yarborough of Texas, received national attention
and resulted in the Bilingual Education Act of 1967.

At the local level, many of the teachers in these
programs have been sought out by different community
agencies to serve as guest speakers, and by local and
national educational agencies as consultants and directors
of workshops in the training of teachers.

Materials

Apparently, there is no one set of materials that
can be utilized at all bilingual schools. Each school is
still seeking instructional materials appropriate to its

local needs and in accordance with cultural and linguistic
considerations. Without exception, many teachers are
creating their own materials, especially in the field of
mathematics. For the most part, these teachers-made
instructional tools are pedagogically sound and should be
collected by a central agency for proper organization and
dissemination. There is a definite need for good materials
at all levels of instruction. So far there are no organized materials to teach the contributions of the ethnic
groups to the advancement of American society, nor is
there a concerted effort being made in this direction by
the teaching staffs.

Library services

Library services ranged from superior to very poor.
Without question, the best organized library was that of
the Garfield Elementary School in Del Rio, Texas. Obviously, the local administration has allocated considerable
funds for the purchase of books and library instructional
materials. The collection of Spanish books is varied and
new. Organization and location of these materials makes
them quite accessible. Instruction via two languages was
observed at the Coral Way Elementary School where a bilingual librarian was able to give instruction on library use
and materials with equal facility in English and Spanish.
Two libraries were quite inadequate from the standpoint of

reading materials. One had eighteen Spanish books and the
other, twenty-three. In both of these libraries, an aide
was in charge.

It appears that if the most salient features of the
two best libraries were combined, the bilingual program
would be more complete in this supportive function. A
bilingual librarian appears to be the best person for
library work since this person is able to extend further
the bilingual instruction philosophy of the school.

Evaluation

At the time that the bilingual programs were initiated, there were no appropriate instruments available for
testing the intelligence and achievement of Spanish-
speaking children. Only within the last two years have
valid testing instruments been created especially for
these children by interested researchers. Superintendent
Brantley of the United Consolidated Independent School
District in Laredo, Texas, points out that he was more
interested in providing every child with an opportunity to
participate in a bilingual program than in having experimental and control sections in his elementary schools back
in 1964 when his program began.[76] Nevertheless, evaluation
procedures have been employed at all of the bilingual programs visited by this writer, except Public School Number
25 in New York City. Public School Number 25 is in its

first year of existence ~~~   have inter-

pretive test dat   ar is over.

Evaluation data   s presented

as follows:

San Antonio Independent School District.--There are

nine elementary schools participating in the bilingual

education program of this system, of which J. T. Bracken-

ridge Elementary School is a part. Results of the program

are as follows:

>   Children participating in the bilingual and
> English-as-a-Second-Language classes have been
> tested using new developmental tests of expressive
> and receptive language, as well as standardized
> I.Q. and achievement tests. Test results show that
> there are highly significant differences between
> pre and post tests for all children tested; chil-
> dren in both bilingual classes and English-as-a-
> Second-Language classes have made significant
> progress during the year in both language develop-
> ment and I.Q. scores.
>   Within the curriculum, analyses show that the
> bilingual version tends to be the better approach
> for vocabulary building and grammar while the
> English-as-a-Second-Language version seems better
> for improving phonology. Emphasis for this year's
> testing program will be on differences between the
> experimental curriculum and the regular SAISD
> curriculum.
>   Future plans call for the expansion of bilin-
> gual education into other schools in SAISD. Of
> particular interest is the possible adaptation of
> the program for use in schools having student
> populations which are predominantly native English
> speakers.
>   San Antonio has long been a bilingual city by
> tradition. All indications are that in the not too
> distant future, the idea of bilingualism will
> become an integral part of the school program.[77]

Nye Elementary School.--Bertha Trevino recently
completed a study at the Nye Elementary School in connection with her Ph.D. dissertation. The title of her study
is "An Analysis of the Effectiveness of a Bilingual Program
in the Teaching of Mathematics in the Primary Grades." Her
conclusions are the following:

> The evidence of this study leads to the conclu-
> sion that the acquisition of a second language does
> not lower the achievement level of the English-
> speaking child in mathematics in the primary grades;
> rather, it facilitates his learning.
> There is abundant evidence in the current
> educational literature that children who feel they
> are in a warm and friendly situation will learn
> more rapidly than children who feel that they are
> in a hostile or strange situation. It may be
> postulated that vernacular teaching lessens a
> child's apprehension and anxiety; thus, the school
> is providing a better opportunity for the Spanish-
> speaking child to learn mathematics. In all cases,
> the scores of the Spanish-speaking child taught
> bilingually were higher than the scores of Spanish-
> speaking children taught exclusively in English.
> The introduction of Spanish in the classroom leads
> to a closer association among all the children.[78]

Coral Way Elementary School.--Another recent study,
also in connection with a Ph.D. dissertation, was done by
Mabel Richardson at the Coral Way Elementary School. The
results of this experiment were reported in Chapter II
under Achievement Studies.

Garfield Elementary School.--A recent evaluation of
the bilingual program at the Garfield Elementary School
provides the following results:

> It would seem that the Garfield experimental
> program can be judged a qualified success./ The
> degree of success is significant if one considers
> that it was a new program, in operation only for
> its first year. /The comparisons of all subjects
> in experimental and control groups showed the
> control subjects to have a superiority in English
> competence but the experimental group showed the
> superior socialization and adjustment. When a
> comparison was made of the two groups including
> only subjects who had been in the program the full
> school year and had not been retained in grade,
> the results showed no significant differences with
> respect to English competence and an even more
> superior socialization for the experimental bilin-
> gual sections. This means that the experimental
> subjects, even though receiving instruction in
> both English and Spanish, were as equally com-
> petent in English as those learning only in
> English. This would seem to be a justification
> for a bilingual program.[79]

The evaluations of these programs seem to indicate
that favorable results are being attained by Spanish-
speaking children who are taught bilingually. In addition,
the acquisition of a second language does not lower the
achievement level of English-speaking children. Both
groups are placed in a learning environment that is conducive to cross-culture appreciation. Taken as a whole,
these evaluations strongly indicate that bilingual programs
are effective and, therefore, justified as a curricular
innovation.

Comments by administrators

One question was posed to all the principals of the bilingual schools. The question was: "What do you consider to be the strongest and the weakest points in your program?"

Among the strong points cited by the principals were the following: (1) adequate planning of time allocated to teachers, (2) a clear, precise statement of objectives, (3) an excellent corps of bilingual staff members, and (4) immediate participation of all students in the program.

Among the weak points cited were: (1) inadequate staffing and materials, (2) weak communication between the staff and the administration, (3) inadequate provision for teacher in-service training, (4) insufficient time for principals to become more involved in the program, and (5) reading and writing in Spanish delayed for Spanish-speaking students.

CHAPTER V

CONCLUSIONS, RECOMMENDATIONS AND GUIDELINES

FOR BILINGUAL PROGRAMS

Summary of Conclusions

This study was made for the purpose of determining
the nature and effectiveness of bilingual education programs for the Spanish-speaking child in the United States.
The number of these programs as of this current school
year is limited to twelve. A news item in the Del Rio
News-Herald (Texas) points to the fact that "there are
only about a dozen programs in the nation which can be
regarded as true bilingual programs."[80] This fact was
confirmed by Albar Peña, Program Advisor in Bilingual
Education, U.S. Office of Education.[81] While this fact
may be hard to accept, one need only to note that the two
largest cities in the United States, New York City and
Chicago, have only one real bilingual program each. The
New York City program serves three-tenths of one per cent
of the 250,000 Puerto Rican children. Chicago's program
is limited to a student enrollment of thirty-five and to
a staff of four teachers. Both programs were initiated

112

in the fall of 1968. Plans in both cities call for one more program to be added in the fall of 1969.

The data used in this study were obtained primarily through two sources. An eight-page questionnaire based on the operational models and strategies discussed in Chapter III formed the basis of the questions. Five of these eight-page questionnaires were distributed to supervisors or directors of bilingual education programs for the Spanish-speaking children in elementary schools. In most cases the information requested was provided by more than one administrative officer as, in some cases, superintendents and principals were just as knowledgeable and interested as the immediate supervisor or director of these programs. The receipt of these questionnaires was followed by an on-the-spot visitation by the researcher.

The writer spent a total of 147 contact hours visiting the five elementary schools reported in this study. The time was spent interviewing administrators, teachers, counselors, nurses, and other supportive personnel. At least one classroom visit was made at each grade level at all the schools. In addition, much of the information reported in this study was acquired through correspondence, telephone calls, and attendance at professional conferences on bilingual education.

Although the study was limited to only five bilin-

gual programs, it is believed that the depth to which
these programs were examined has provided interesting and
informative data concerning the operational theories and
practices similar to the majority of so-called "real"
bilingual education programs. The programs chosen for
this study represent the three major Spanish-speaking
ethnic groups in the United States: the Cubans, the Puerto
Ricans, and the Mexican-Americans. Within the limitations
of this study, it appears that the Coral Way Elementary
School bilingual program is the best in the United States.
This is to be expected as this program was the first of
its kind in this country and has had time to work out
solutions to most of its problems of scheduling, staffing,
supervision, coordination, materials, etc. The three
Texas programs are in different stages of development.
The Nye Elementary School program is the best of these
three programs. In New York City, Public School No. 25,
The Bilingual School, was begun only last fall and, while
it is beset with all the problems inherent in a new program, it is meeting a local need in an efficient manner.

The in-depth examinations of these programs via
questionnaire and on-the-spot visitation yielded insights
as to the most generalizable features of these programs.
The most essential information relative to these programs
is restated below. Following the summary will be found a

list of recommendations and guidelines for bilingual programs.

Theoretical considerations

The recent interest in bilingual education has been mostly in the area of philosophical, sociological, psychological, and linguistic considerations. Without a doubt, the theory underlying bilingual education has been well established and accepted by American educators who face the problem of providing this type of education for non-English-speaking pupils in our public and parochial schools. The national interest has been such as to encourage the enactment of the Bilingual Education Act, based mostly on the Senate hearings on bilingual education conducted by the Special Subcommittee on Bilingual Education of the Committee on Labor and Public Welfare in May, June, and July of 1967. Testimony by most of the prominent scholars and educators in this area resulted in the acceptance of bilingual education theory and practice as a solution to the low achievement of non-English-speaking children in our public schools.

Successful results

Based on the evaluation of these programs by local and non-local agencies, the effectiveness of these programs has been clearly established. Spanish-speaking

children finally have been provided a type of two-language
instruction which has resulted in greater mastery of
speaking, reading, and writing than under the conventional
English tongue medium of instruction. The retention of
students over longer sequences of school attendance has
also come about.

Perhaps the best indication of the success of these
programs is evidenced by the increase in number of new
programs in different parts of the country. The recent
submission of over three hundred proposals to the U.S.
Office of Education for federal funding is additional
evidence. This evidence is highly significant as over
25 per cent of these programs are likely to be funded.
New York and Chicago introduced bilingual programs for the
first time during the fall of 1968 and will expand their
offering in the coming school years.

The general feeling among most educators of the
non-English-speaking is that we are at last near a solution for the educational problems of these children.
Community acceptance has become more prevalent everywhere.

Inherent problems

The usual problems of materials, evaluation procedures, teacher training, recruitment, financing, etc.,
continue to be chief concerns for advocates of these
programs. Also, the inability to do away with duplication

of efforts in materials selection, preparation, and dissemination remains a problem. Each bilingual program
operates independently of the others; hence, sharing of
materials and ideas really has not been practiced to the
extent that it could be.

Educators are still looking for answers to the
problems of placement, articulation, and better testing
devices for specific ethnic groups. Radio and television
have been neglected as partial answers to the transmission
of instruction via a central control station.

Future expectations

At least in the immediate foreseeable future,
bilingual education will continue to be accepted on a
more national basis than has been the case during the
short six years of this current new curricular innovation.
The social trends of the times have aided this movement
considerably. The Bilingual Education Act will likely be
expanded to provide more services to the linguistically
handicapped in a broader context. The number of EPDA
institutes for the training and retraining of teachers
for bilingual programs has increased and will continue to
increase as colleges and universities expand their curricula to provide a strong program of pre- and in-service
training for prospective and established teachers.

A cadre of better trained teaching and adminis-

trative personnel from the ethnic groups is now being
developed and will ultimately accept greater responsibility in the administration of these programs.

The ultimate future of these programs, indeed the
entire movement, will depend on the quality of the programs
themselves. It will be up to them to exhibit a sufficient
quality to overcome the reservations of critical observers
in our communities. Somehow, the public must be made to
feel that this is neither a passing fad nor a panacea, but
rather an innovation that is based on sound theory and
sound practice, and that it is perhaps the best, if not
the only, answer to a problem that has long perplexed
American educators.

Recommendations

School policy

1. The standard form of the language (Spanish
and/or English) should be taught as the dialect which is
appropriate for school, community, and other uses without
discouraging the student's own dialect which is appropriate
for use with his intimate friends and in the family circle.[82]

2. Bilingual education should be provided through
the mediums of Spanish and English throughout the entire
language arts program in the elementary school, including
music, art, and physical education.

3. Professionally trained Cubans, Puerto Ricans, and Mexican-Americans should be given a greater voice in running schools where the majority of the school enrollment is Spanish-speaking. This will mean, among other things, that Latin American teachers, teacher aides, administrators, clerks, cooks, janitors, etc., should represent the ethnic group in the general school operation.

4. School board representation by Latin Americans should be proportional to the number of Spanish-speaking children in the community.

5. Every effort should be made to stimulate and encourage the emergence of native leaders in each ethnic group of the community.

6. In communities where large numbers of Spanish-speaking pupils make up the majority of a school enrollment, a specialist (Spanish-speaking preferably) should be appointed to serve as liaison between the dominant group in the community and the Spanish-speaking community. This specialist should be a high-echelon administrative officer from the board of education.

7. An effort should be made to assign teachers in elementary grades who have studied Spanish, along with the prescribed courses in elementary education, since such teachers would more readily understand errors in pronunciation in English which carry over from the Spanish language.

8. If possible, counselors with a Spanish-speaking background should be assigned to those schools where large concentrations of Spanish-speaking children are present.

9. Careful recruiting and screening procedures should be employed so as to select only those teachers who desire to take a personal interest in the bilingual program.

10. Bilingual children should be put in personal contact with good human models in their own cultural tradition since such personal contact is helpful to the bilingual's self-image.

11. Both bilingual children and parents may profit from the use of exemplary persons from Latin American countries when the local school board can use them in the community for drama, music, speaking, and sports.

12. The fine Latin American family system should be used to establish communication between the school and the home through the Spanish language.

13. The results of all pertinent attempts at solving particular problems of bilingual education should be made known to all of those interested and means for the dissemination of this information should be devised.

14. Research at all levels of instruction and subject matter should be encouraged. Ideas and materials resulting from this research should be collected and then

shared by teachers or administrators in the bilingual
program.

15. Foreign travel and study in Spanish-speaking
countries for teachers in bilingual programs should be
encouraged and subsidized, if possible.

16. Provision should be made for those teachers in
bilingual programs who wish to attend related professional
meetings, conferences, and in-service training sessions
which take place during the regular school day.

Materials

1. As there is no one set of materials that is
adequate for all bilingual programs, each school should
attempt to develop its own materials while at the same
time adapting, if possible, those that are used in other
programs.

2. Materials brought in from Spanish-speaking
countries must be adapted carefully for (a) pattern drills
to move from a non-standard to a standard dialect, (b) re-
sequencing to correspond more closely to the sequence and
content of the English language courses, and (c) special
introductory listening and speaking practice materials for
the mother tongue of children who retain no skill other
than minimum aural comprehension.[83]

3. The development, trial use, or demonstration of
self-instructional materials designed specifically to teach

standard English or Spanish to speakers of non-standard
dialects should be encouraged.

4. If possible, a bilingual librarian should be in
charge of finding, ordering, and cataloguing as many Spanish reading books as possible. Filmstrips, sound tapes,
and slides should be part of the library collection.
Newspapers and magazines in Spanish should also be included.
Instruction on the use of the library as well as library
reading sessions should be equally divided in English and
Spanish.

5. An exchange of materials between programs should
be initiated and carried out on a continuing basis.

6. Materials developed within a school system
should be collected and made available to those teachers
who may not be particularly creative. This will encourage
and facilitate lesson planning and subsequent instruction
by grade level or by subject matter.

7. A program of language development--recording,
writing, and publication in the Spanish tongue--should
begin at once, dealing both with Latin American history,
religion, lore, folk tales, points of view on current
problems, etc., and with the essential subject matter of
the school curriculum.

8. In order to encourage the development of the
self-image and pride in ethnic culture, a program of

development of the contributions of the Cubans, Puerto
Ricans, and Mexican-Americans to American culture should
be begun on a national basis. To date these materials are
few and inadequate.

Methodology

1. For both languages the chief way to assure
meaningful practice will always be to use each as a medium
of instruction, rather than to have it studied as an end
in itself.[84]

2. There should be an establishment of complete
curriculum-wide literacy programs in the mother tongue of
bilingual children. These might vary widely as to beginning level, number of grade levels started simultaneously,
amount of time devoted to instruction in and through the
mother tongue.[85]

3. An on-going re-evaluation of the reading methods
and techniques in the primary and intermediate grades
should be made.

4. Programs based upon activity rather than the
traditional type should be more widely instituted, particularly where the Spanish-speaking students are in the
majority.

5. A pre-first-grade experience other than the
traditional kindergarten should be established for Spanish-

speaking pupils who are not prepared to function effectively in either kindergarten or first grade.

6. In order to facilitate later success in the
manipulation of English, Spanish-speaking children should
be made literate in Spanish first.

7. To insure that Spanish will be taught at an
effective level for the development of the bilinguals,
some of the school subjects should be taught in Spanish
from the beginning.[86]

8. Both languages should be learned through the
acquisition of deeply ingrained speech habits resulting
from immense amounts of meaningful listening and oral practice.[87]

9. Functional improvement in reading and writing
must be based on corresponding levels of habitual listening and speaking. The four skills (listening, speaking,
reading, and writing) should reinforce each other through
careful planning of learning activities and procedures of
introduction.

10. For those Spanish-speaking children who have or
may be expected to have special difficulty with English,
English should be taught as a second language, and Spanish
should be taught as a mother tongue or native language.[88]

11. In schools where only a part of the pupils are
Spanish-speaking, instead of the full 50-50 bilingual

program, there should be at least one hour of instruction
per day through the medium of the Spanish language,
designed to reinforce all areas of the school curriculum
in grades 1-6. The purpose of this recommendation is to
avoid retardation, strengthen the home-school relationship,
and enhance the child's self-image.

12. In those schools where complete programs of
study through Spanish cannot be established for the benefit
of the Spanish-speaking pupils, Spanish classes should be
taught in a different way (Spanish for the Spanish-
speaking).[89]

13. Content courses (World History, Geography,
Sociology, etc.) at the fourth-, fifth-, or sixth-grade
level should be taught entirely through the medium of
Spanish in order to take the place of, or as alternatives
to, the customary advanced-level terminal language
courses.[90]

Evaluation

1. Administrators, counselors, and testing personnel should seek out, or adapt, or create tests which will
most satisfactorily determine a more accurate showing of
the potentiality of Spanish-speaking pupils. The Anglo-
slanted instruments of evaluation are simply not appropriate for these children.

2. Teachers and guidance personnel should be aware of Spanish-speaking students whose standardized test scores are high, but whose grades are lower.

3. Teachers should be encouraged to recognize the academically talented Spanish-speaking child and help develop the talents he has. This will require judgments other than those based on tests.

4. Personnel responsible for selecting the most proper testing instruments for the Spanish-speaking child should (a) contact the regional educational development centers, (b) seek the help of colleges and universities, and (c) acquire testing instruments from the ministries of education of the many Spanish-speaking countries. Recent developments in the creation of newer and more sophisticated testing instruments are now under way in many parts of the world.[91]

Teacher training

1. Colleges and universities should provide special training, pre- and in-service, to those individuals who wish to teach in a bilingual program. This would require a revamping of current curricular offerings.

2. Prospective teachers of bilingual children should be required to have more than a smattering of sociology studies. Some courses should be in the area of Latin American culture.

3. Teachers of bilingual education programs should have training in the psychology and motivation of disadvantaged children.

4. A number of courses dealing with the contributions of the ethnic groups to American culture should be included to help the teacher of the disadvantaged Spanish-speaking youth.

5. Theory of working with Spanish-speaking youth should be related to daily problems faced by teachers, especially when the previous training of these teachers has afforded them inadequate preparation for the language teaching the situation demands.

6. Anglos preparing to teach in a bilingual program should be required to take several courses of Spanish and Latin American culture in order to understand better the world of the disadvantaged Latin American child.

7. Definite course requirements for teachers in the bilingual program should be: Teaching English as a Foreign Language and the Structure of English.

8. In addition to the elementary curriculum courses, a separate reading course concerned with the special problems of bilingual children should be required. This course should have a strong linguistic orientation.

9. Actual observation and opportunity to work closely with bilingual children should be a definite

requirement for prospective teachers in bilingual education programs.

10. Native speakers of Spanish educated in Spanish outside the United States should be trained in a language arts approach to teaching.

11. Native speakers of Spanish educated in the United States should be given special courses in Spanish to give them greater confidence in the use and teaching of this language.

12. Already effective classroom teachers are good candidates for English as a Second Language programs and should be recruited for this purpose when specially trained personnel are not available.

13. Although there are not many teachers who have been trained in college for teaching in a bi-cultural situation, local school boards should attempt to secure the services of these persons when available.

14. The number of EPDA institutes now in existence (less than 10) for special in-service training for teachers in bilingual schools should be increased and improved.

15. A vigorous in-service training program for teachers at the local level should be provided through workshops utilizing local and outside leaders.

Research

1. Research should be conducted in areas where large numbers of Spanish-speaking students reside, so that measures may be taken by the school district to help correct problems in the schools and in the community.

2. Research should be focused on the history, languages, and culture of the Latin Americans in the United States.

3. Research should be initiated to determine why some Spanish-speaking students achieve academically. This information should then be used to set up programs to help those who have potential but whose performance and achievement are not as great.

4. Survey-type research on the nature and effectiveness of bilingual education programs should be conducted periodically to check the progress of this curricular innovation for the Spanish-speaking students.

5. Research to measure the achievement of bilinguals in all areas of the language arts program, including art, music, and physical education, should be continued. The number of such experiments has been few, and the dissemination of the results has not been carried out nationally.

Guidelines for Setting Up an Exemplary
Bilingual Program

1. Form a planning committee representative of the
key people in the community who have had experience and
who understand the difference between transitional and real
bilingual education programs.

2. Select or hire administrative personnel who will
give their unconditional support to the bilingual program.

3. Every effort should be made to select sympa-
thetic administrative officers and teachers for schools
with bilingual programs.

4. Make the school an all-bilingual school. Children whose parents do not want them in the program should
be assigned to other nearby schools.[92]

5. Prepare a statement of desired objectives and
make sure to state them in behavioral terms. This will
assure planning consistent with predetermined goals and
provide a source of constant check on progress.

6. Select instructional staffing that meets the
local situation: two sets of monolinguals (one English and
one Spanish) or one set of bilinguals to form the teaching
staff.

7. Select within the system those teachers who can
adjust to the organizational pattern and whose concern for
the bilingual child will make them accept the reality of
more work rather than less. New personnel should meet the

same requirements of adaptability and personal concern.

8.   Since bilingual education programs require more than average time for planning lessons among grades and subjects, the teaching staff should be provided with at least one hour per day to do such planning. Work space should be provided along with the allotment of time.

9.   The student body should be divided into at least three groups: those who are non-English-speaking, those who are non-Spanish-speaking, and those who are bilingual. In a bilingual school this takes precedence over ability grouping.

10.   Make a special effort to provide for articulation between grades and between tracks, as stated above.

11.   The amount of time devoted to the vernacular and to the second tongue should be flexible and depend on the needs of each grouping of students as indicated in Item 9, and should include instruction throughout the language arts, science, mathematics, music, and physical education.

12.   Pick two language specialists in the area of Teaching English as a Second Language and Teaching Spanish as a Second Language. The use of these specialists will facilitate a placement service function for new students who transfer into the program.

13.   Since a bilingual school demands more than

average cooperation at all levels, create a good communication system within the school. Every person involved in
the program should be informed of all aspects of the
operation and should discharge his assigned duty with a
seriousness of purpose.

14. Assign to the bilingual program only teachers
who are understanding, kind, and patient. These teachers
should be interested in bilingual education and should be
able to work closely with their colleagues. In addition,
these teachers should be creative in the use of audio-
visual aids and in directing activity-oriented learning
experiences.

15. Select a director of curriculum who is bilingual
so that he can understand the needs of speakers of both
languages. This individual should have the bilingual point
of view and should endeavor to learn and understand the
culture of the second language groups.

16. Appoint a supervisor of the bilingual program
who is preferably a bilingual and who is himself a master
teacher. This person should be free to carry out public
relations functions in and away from the community.

17. Appoint a bilingual visiting teacher-counselor
who can communicate effectively with the parents in the
community.

18. Set up a budget allowance for second language

books, materials, equipment, library books, salaries for aides and consultant services.[93]

19. Allocate library space that is adequate for this purpose. The librarian and her assistant should be bilingual and should give the children instruction in the use of the library and related services (story telling, movies, recordings) through the two languages.

20. Employ a music teacher and an art teacher who are bilingual, or who have a bilingual aide assigned to them.[94]

21. As most regions have a source of bilinguals in the community, select persons who are bilingual and who have a personal stake in the program. In many cases aides are qualified to do more than non-instructional duties, such as helping children with reading, mathematics, spelling, etc.

22. Employ bilingual personnel for the school office.

23. Since the bilingual school will be on public exhibit most of the time, select teachers who can maintain poise while being observed by visitors. This will require persons who are able to stand up and teach and who do not mind having their work on exhibit at all times and without advance notice.

24. Hire, if possible, bilingual supportive personnel such as cooks, janitors, clerks, etc.

25. Provide for the teaching staff a regular in-
service training program within the school, locally and
system-wide.

26. Before the program starts, conduct a summer
workshop for training new personnel and for retooling
others.

27. Encourage the local college or university to
provide special courses for teachers of bilingual schools,
preferably leading to advanced degrees, or at least toward
salary increments.

28. Encourage teachers to visit other bilingual
programs, attend EPDA summer institutes, and to travel and
study abroad.

29. Since community support is so essential to these
programs, sell the idea to the PTA first. Be cooperative
with the local press. Offer some type of second language
instruction for parents so that they may understand better
the intent of the program.[95]

30. Enlist the support of social, business, and
religious agencies in the community.

31. Provide for on-going evaluation of the program.
In addition to local evaluation procedures, make provision
for outside evaluation.

32. Keep accurate records on student achievement and progress throughout the school year and over the years.

33. Invite interested scholars to make use of the bilingual school for experimentation purposes.

REFERENCES

[1]Albar Peña, Program Advisor, Bilingual Education Section, U.S. Office of Education, personal telephone communication, April 29, 1969.

[2]Reports of the Working Committee, Foreign Language Teaching: Challenges to the Profession (The Northeast Conference on the Teaching of Foreign Languages, 1965), p. 57.

[3]Ibid.

[4]Mildred Boyer, "Bilingual Schooling: A Dimension of Democracy," Texas Foreign Language Association Bulletin, Vol. II (December, 1968), p. 1.

[5]Elementary and Secondary Education Act Amendment of 1967, Title VII: Bilingual Education Act, P.L. 90-247.

[6]A. Bruce Gaarder, "Organization of the Bilingual School," The Journal of Social Issues, Vol. XXXIII (April, 1967), p. 110.

[7]Dorothy D. Duhon, "Colorado Report on Education for Bilingual Children," Reports: Bilingual Education-- Research and Teaching (Annual Conference of the Southwest Council of Foreign Language Teachers, 1967), p. 66.

[8]A. Bruce Gaarder, Addresses and Reports presented at the Conference on Development of Bilingualism in Children of Varying Linguistic and Cultural Heritages, sponsored by Regional Educational Agencies Project in International Education, Texas Education Agency, Austin, Texas, January 31, 1967, p. 1.

[9]Ibid., pp. 2-3.

[10]Ibid., p. 10.

[11]Harold Howe, II, "Cowboys, Indians, and American Education," The Texas Outlook, Vol. LII (June, 1968), pp. 13, 25.

[12]Ralph W. Yarborough, "Bilingual Education as a Social Force," Foreign Language Annals, Vol. II (March, 1969), p. 327.

[13]The Florida Foreign Language Reporter (January, 1965), p. 18.

[14]Herschel T. Manuel, Addresses and Reports presented at the Conference on Development of Bilingualism in Children of Varying Linguistic and Cultural Heritages, sponsored by Regional Educational Agencies Project in International Education, Texas Education Agency, Austin, Texas, January 31, 1967, pp. 66-67.

[15]Pauline M. Rojas, "Instructional Materials and Aids to Facilitate Teaching the Bilingual Child," Modern Language Journal, Vol. XLIX (February, 1965), p. 237.

[16]Donald D. Walsh, "Bilingualism and Bilingual Education: A Guest Editorial," Foreign Language Annals, Vol. II (March, 1969), p. 298.

[17]William G. Carr, U.S. Senate, Committee on Labor and Public Welfare, Hearings Before the Special Subcommittee on Bilingual Education, Part 1, 90th Cong., 1st Sess., 1967, p. 89.

[18]Gaarder, The Journal of Social Issues, op. cit., p. 110.

[19]Joshua A. Fishman, "The Implications of Bilingualism for Language Teaching and Language Learning," Trends in Language Teaching, edited by Albert Valdman (New York: McGraw-Hill Company, 1966), p. 126.

[20]E. Glyn Lewis, "Language and Language Development," Bilingualism in the Schools of Wales (Swansea, Wales: Welsh Department, Ministry of Education, University College, January, 1962), pp. 9-16.

[21]Donald D. Walsh, "Too Little and Too Late," Modern Language Journal, Vol. XLIX (March, 1965), p. 83.

[22]Mildred Donoghue, "A Rationale for FLES," French Review, Vol. XXXVIII (February, 1965), p. 523.

[23]Theodore Andersson, "Bilingual Schooling: Oasis or Mirage?" Hispania, Vol. LII (March, 1969), p. 69.

[24]John B. Carroll, "The Contributions of Psychological Theory and Educational Research to the Teaching of Foreign Languages," Trends in Language Teaching, edited by Albert Valdman (New York: McGraw-Hill Book Company, 1966), pp. 101-102.

[25]Ibid., pp. 104-105.

[26]Ibid., pp. 105-106.

[27]Nelson Brooks, "The Meaning of Bilingualism Today," Foreign Language Annals, Vol. II (March, 1969), p. 307.

[28]Robert Lado, "Our Bilinguals: Linguistic and Pedagogical Barriers," Reports: Our Bilinguals (Annual Conference of the Southwest Council of Foreign Language Teachers, 1965), p. 15.

[29]Ibid.

[30]A. Bruce Gaarder, "Our Bilinguals: Linguistic and Pedagogical Barriers," Reports: Our Bilinguals (Annual Conference of the Southwest Council of Foreign Language Teachers, 1965), p. 17.

[31]John M. Sharp, "Our Bilinguals: Linguistic and Pedagogical Barriers," Reports: Our Bilinguals (Annual Conference of the Southwest Council of Foreign Language Teachers, 1965), pp. 27-28.

[32]Ibid., p. 28.

[33]Ibid.

[34]Ibid.

[35]Carmen Slominski, The Relationship of Bilingualism to School Achievement (unpublished seminar report, The Ohio State University, 1968), p. 1.

[36]Donald D. Walsh, "Longer and Better: The Foreign Language Sequence," Modern Language Journal, Vol. LII (November, 1968), p. 428.

[37]Walsh, Foreign Language Annals, op. cit., p. 301.

[38]Mabel Wilson Richardson, "An Evaluation of Certain Aspects of the Academic Achievement of Elementary Pupils in a Bilingual Program" (unpublished Ph.D. dissertation, University of Miami, 1968), pp. 61-62.

[39]Ibid., pp. 63-64.

[40]Claude M. Ury, "The Bilingual Education Act--Bridge to Understanding," The Catholic School Journal, Vol. 68 (September, 1968), p. 33.

[41]Ibid.

[42]Yarborough, Foreign Language Annals, op. cit., p. 325.

[43]Albar Peña, op. cit.

[44]Ury, op. cit.

[45]Walsh, Foreign Language Annals, op. cit., pp. 298-299.

[46]Gaarder, The Journal of Social Issues, op. cit., p. 111.

[47]Boyer, op. cit., p. 1.

[48]Elementary and Secondary Education Act Amendment of 1967, Title VII: Bilingual Education Act, P.L. 90-247.

[49]Boyer, op. cit., p. 2.

[50]Gaarder, Conference on Development of Bilingualism in Children of Varying Linguistic and Cultural Heritages, op. cit., p. 7.

[51]Sam Frank Cheavens, "Vernacular Languages and Education" (unpublished Ph.D. dissertation, The University of Texas, 1957), p. 5.

[52]Yarborough, op. cit., p. 325.

[53]Boyer, op. cit., pp. 3-5.

[54]Gaarder, The Journal of Social Issues, op. cit., p. 110.

[55]Gaarder, Conference on Development of Bilingualism in Children of Varying Linguistic and Cultural Heritages, op. cit., p. 4.

[56]Ibid.

[57]Gaarder, The Journal of Social Issues, op. cit., p. 111.

[58]Southeastern Education Laboratory, Razon de Ser of the Bilingual School, Atlanta, Georgia, n.d., Foreword.

[59]Ibid., p. 1.

[60]Ibid., p. 2.

[61]Ibid.

[62]Ibid., p. 3.

[63]Ibid.

[64]Ibid., p. 4.

[65]Gaarder, Conference on Development of Bilingualism in Children of Varying Linguistic and Cultural Heritages, op. cit., p. 4.

[66]Dr. Albar Pena, Program Advisor, Bilingual Section, U.S. Office of Education; Mr. Armando Rodríquez, Chief, Mexican-American Affairs Unit, U.S. Office of Education; and Dr. Theodore Andersson, Director, USOE Bilingual Design, Southwest Educational Development Laboratory, Austin, Texas.

[67]Joseph Murphy, "The Contributions of Social Studies Methodology to Foreign Language Teaching" (unpublished Ph.D. dissertation, The Ohio State University, 1968), pp. 14-36.

[68]Arnold Raisner, Philip Bolger, and Carmen Sanguinetti, Science Instruction in Spanish for Pupils of Spanish-Speaking Background (Office of Educational Research, Board of Education of the City of New York, 1967).

[69]"Commonwealth of Puerto Rico," Encyclopedia Americana, 1969, XXII, 799.

[70]Joshua A. Fishman, Robert L. Cooper, Roxana Ma et al., Bilingualism in the Barrio (Final Report: Yeshiva University, Contract No. OEC-1-7-062816-0297, U.S. Department of Health, Education and Welfare, 1968), pp. 8-10.

[71]Ibid.

[72]Elmer Bendiner, "Outside the Kingdom of the Middle Class," The Nation, Vol. CCIV (January 2, 1967), pp. 22-23.

[73]Armando Rodriquez, Chief, Mexican-American Affairs Unit, U.S. Office of Education, personal interview, February 16, 1969.

[74]Report of the NEA-Tucson Survey on the Teaching of Spanish to the Spanish-Speaking, The Invisible Minority (Washington, D.C.: National Education Association, 1966), p. 10.

[75]Josué González, "Bilingual Program Involves 4,000 Students," San Antonio Independent School District, Our Schools, Vol. XXI (November, 1968), p. 2.

[76]Harold Brantley, Superintendent of the United Consolidated Independent School District, personal interview, March 10, 1969.

[77]González, op. cit., pp. 3-4.

[78]Bertha Treviño, "An Analysis of the Effectiveness of a Bilingual Program in the Teaching of Mathematics in the Primary Grades" (unpublished Ph.D. dissertation, The University of Texas at Austin, 1968), pp. 98-99.

[79]Del Rio Independent School District (Texas), An Evaluation of the Garfield Experimental Program in Bilingual Education, March, 1969.

[80]Dan Bus, "The Bi-lingual Approach: Del Rio Technique," Del Rio News-Herald, Section B, Sunday, March 23, 1969, pp. 1-2.

[81]Pena, op. cit.

[82]Lado, op. cit., p. 15.

[83]Southwest Council of Foreign Language Teachers, Reports: Our Bilinguals, 1965, pp. 24-25.

[84] Gaarder, <u>Reports: Our Bilinguals</u>, op. cit., p. 19.

[85] Southwest Council of Foreign Language Teachers, op. cit., p. 24.

[86] Lado, op. cit., p. 15.

[87] Ibid.

[88] Gaarder, <u>Reports: Our Bilinguals</u>, op. cit., p. 19.

[89] Southwest Council of Foreign Language Teachers, op. cit., p. 25.

[90] Ibid.

[91] Ibid.

[92] J. L. Logan, "Recommendations for Planning a Bilingual Program," part of a paper presented to the Conference on the Conservation of Bilingual Resources, University of Michigan, Ann Arbor, March 18, 1967.

[93] Ibid.

[94] Ibid.

[95] Ibid.

APPENDIXES

APPENDIX A

RADIO AND TELEVISION

Within the limitations of this study, it has
been noted that radio and television media are not being
utilized to their fullest potential in bilingual schools.
In most cases they are not being used at all for basic
presentation or for enrichment. It is surprising that
even along the Mexican border, in Laredo and Del Rio,
where telecasting in Spanish is commonplace, no utilization of the media is being made. In light of this
information, the following recommendations and suggestions are made specifically for the integration of radio
and television in bilingual programs:

1. It is advisable that plans be made to experiment with radio and television for both basic presentation
and enrichment.

2. A cooperative effort should be made between the
commercial stations and the local school systems to make
Spanish programming available to children in bilingual
programs. Suggested programming could be cartoons, short
stories, historical excerpts, book reviews, etc.

3. Sometime during the school day, children should

144

be exposed to 15-20 minutes of Spanish program viewing for enrichment purposes.

4. School districts with television facilities should invite local schools to present special programs for telecasting to all schools in the district and to the general public. This would result in better community relations.

5. While most of the programs visited have a special component of music in both English and Spanish, this is one activity that could definitely be supplemented by television. Much of the present entertainment on television already lends itself to this usage.

6. The use of episodic narratives would provide excellent practice in listening to both English and Spanish speakers. This type of programming already is a mainstay of commercial television.

7. The best models of Spanish pronunciation are usually heard on radio and television. Children should be exposed to these models. This activity would provide them discrimination practice when they are privileged to listen to more than one voice.

8. As applies especially to the use of radio, there is no reason why selected listening activities might not be used for whole class participation. Dependency on sound alone could do much to develop sound discrimination and train for the skill of listening.

9. Special programs should be developed for bilingual children at the elementary school level. The type of listening program developed by Alan Garfinkel at The Ohio State University could do much to promote general interest and involvement.

10. The school board should make an honest, direct effort to involve the parents in the bilingual program. Some definitive suggestions for this would be to promote a series of programs aimed at monolingual, Spanish-speaking parents who are only vaguely aware of the role of the school in the lives of their children. Programs to be developed could be those dealing with the following topics: Our Public Schools, Our Health Program, The Counseling Services, The Adult Education Program, etc. The language of these programs would be Spanish, of course.

11. Micro-teaching is now being used in at least one bilingual program, that of the San Antonio Independent School District, where three portable units are available to the supervisors for recording the performance of new and experienced teachers. The simplicity of playback has provided the classroom teacher with an immediate recording of her teaching. This teacher training aid should be utilized in other programs.

APPENDIX B

TEACHER EDUCATION

The problem of training teachers for bilingual
programs is easily the most pressing one at the present
time. Most of the programs visited in Texas were, however,
fortunate in having easy access to a potential source--
the Mexican-American, who is a natural bilingual. As
might be suspected, the number of bilingual teachers needed
(100,000 according to Rodriquez, Chief of the Mexican-
American Affairs Unit in Washington) is not being met. In
order to provide this corps of trained staff, the local
universities must accept more and more responsibility in
training programs. What can be done is outlined below:

1. Local school systems must take an even greater
part in providing in-service training for teachers already
on the job. These workshops will have to be given after
school, on weekends, and during the summer months.

2. Local colleges and universities can provide
assistance by offering two types of in-service training:

a) A commuters institute for teachers who are
unable to leave their families over a prolonged period of
time. Currently, this need is being met at Our Lady of

147

the Lake College in San Antonio, Texas. Teachers who are working in schools where there are large concentrations of Mexican-American pupils and where English is taught as a second language have been accepted into a weekend-type EPDA Institute. These classes are held every Friday evening from 4:30 to 9:30 P.M. and on Saturdays from 8:00 A.M. to 5:00 P.M. Participants are paid a stipend. Courses offered are the following: Applied Spanish Linguistics, Intermediate and Advanced Oral Spanish, English as a Second Language, Literature Study, Demonstration Classes (with an opportunity to participate, followed by peer and supervisor critique), Materials Evaluation, Lectures, Seminars, etc.

b) EPDA Summer Institutes for Bilingual Teachers and Aides. A check of institutes of this type as reported by the Modern Language Journal reveals that there are only four to be held during the summer of 1969: one each in Arizona and California; two in Texas. The Institute at the University of Texas in the summer of 1968 provided the following curriculum:

Advanced undergraduate instruction in Civilization of Spanish America, including history, geography, literature, and the arts, in about equal proportions.

A six-credit graduate course in Educational Curriculum and Instruction on Elementary School Bilingual Education. This course provided a sound theoretical basis for effective teaching in Spanish of the elementary school subjects.

A workshop consisting of two parts: (1) design
and demonstration of various formats of bilingual
education in the elementary school; (2) development of methods and materials for the Spanish part
of bilingual teaching.

Special instruction to aid participants in
upgrading their use of Spanish.

Special conferences on such topics which sug-
gest objectives, possible curricular models,
instructional techniques, lists of materials in
Spanish for each elementary subject for each
grade, evaluation instruments, and suggested
recommendations to school boards, school administrators, teachers, parents, and children.

A series of lectures and seminar discussions
by outstanding educational leaders especially
knowledgeable in the field of bilingual (Spanish-
English elementary education.

3. Year-long EPDA Institutes to prepare leadership

for the bilingual education program. This type of insti-

tute would be similar to the NDEA type with full course

work and stipend for participant and dependents.

4. Major universities such as Florida State at

Tallahassee, The Ohio State University, New York University

--all with established doctoral programs in foreign lan-

guage education--should offer their doctoral candidates

special training in bilingual education.

5. Beginning as soon as possible, teachers of

bilingual programs should be provided the opportunity for

foreign study in the country where Spanish is spoken

natively. Activities in conjunction with bilingual pro-

grams in these countries would bring the participants into

contact with new ideas and approaches in teaching the
bilingual child.

6. Pre-Service Instruction. Our Lady of the Lake
College in San Antonio has started a pre-service training
program for future teachers of bilingual education. This
program, called Project Teacher Excellence, trains young,
dedicated men and women who already know by the first or
second year in college that they wish to become teachers
in bilingual programs. Under this plan, students are
assigned part-time duties to those schools in the San
Antonio area which have bilingual programs. The students
work as aides to regular teachers and thus acquire first-
hand experiences in real situations.

7. Teacher Recruitment. It is ironic that while
we speak of a serious shortage of bilingual teachers,
there is a great potential already existent in those areas
where bilingual programs are in progress. An intensive
recruitment of Cubans, Puerto Ricans, and Mexican-Americans
needs to be undertaken to take advantage of a national
resource. Also, the returnees from the Peace Corps in
Latin American countries are another source of talent.

MATERIALS (ANNOTATED)

Garfield Elementary School
(Del Rio, Texas)

Grades 1 and 2

MacRae, Margit W. Mi Cuaderno de español, Book I. Boston:
Houghton Mifflin Co., 1959. 48 pp.
   This workbook is planned to accompany the
teacher's manual, Spanish in the Grades, Book One,
by Margit MacRae. Together they provide effective
instruction in hearing and speaking Spanish and
initiate a foundation for reading, writing, and
cross-cultural understanding. Book One contains
3 folk tales familiar to all children, which are
used to develop vocabulary and language skills.
The teacher's manual has patterns for the visual
aids that are needed. Lesson plans are given for
each week of the school year. The workbook has
simple stories to read and pictures to color.

   . Mi Cuaderno de español, Book II. Boston:
Houghton Mifflin Co., 1960. 48 pp.
   This is the second workbook of the series
Spanish in the Grades and is used in conjunction
with the teacher's manual, Book Two. It expands
the vocabulary and skills introduced in Book One.
The teacher's edition contains daily lesson plans
for the entire year as well as patterns for the
visual aids. The Appendix has a Spanish-English
Word List and the songs and games that provide
practice patterns.
   There are five phonograph records, Sing and
Speak Spanish, which accompany Margit MacRae's
Spanish in the Grades and support the audio-lingual
approach to teaching.

Pastor, Angeles; Vda. de Capo, Rosa Guzman; Tejera, Carmen
  Gómez; and Hester, Kathleen B. <u>Amigos de aquí y de</u>
  <u>allá</u> (Libro Primero). Illustrated by Beth Wilson.
  River Forest, Ill.: Laidlaw Brothers, Inc., 1961.
  128·pp.
      <u>Amigos de aquí y de allá</u> is the fourth book
  in the series <u>Por el mundo del cuento y la aventura</u>,
  a series of basic readers developed under the
  auspices of the Department of Public Instruction
  of Puerto Rico. It follows a readiness book and
  two pre-primers. It is composed of four topical
  sections of stories and games for beginning readers.
  Each section is followed by one or two pages of
  review material. The teacher's manual has suggestions for presenting the lessons and practice and
  enrichment activities for the pupils.

Quintero, Gregorio Torres. <u>Método Onomatopéyico</u>. México,
  D.F., Editorial Patria, S.A. (Primer Cuatrimestre,
  50 pp., Segundo Cuatrimestre, 46 pp.).
      In this book the onomatopoeic method is used.
  Each letter is heard, pronounced, identified as an
  element of a word, seen, read, and written by the
  pupil.

Scott, Tirsa Saavedra. <u>Somos Amigos, Libro Primero</u>.
  Boston: Ginn and Company, 1964. 124 pp.
      <u>Somos Amigos</u> is designed to teach the two
  language skills of listening comprehension and
  speaking, using the pattern approach with emphasis
  on the audio-lingual-visual method of teaching. As
  pupils develop oral mastery of the language, reading
  is gradually introduced. Each unit is followed by
  an oral review made up of questions and answers in
  past tenses in Spanish. The narrative text is
  interspersed with dialogues, dramatizations,
  jingles, games, and songs to provide interesting
  drills. A teacher's manual has detailed suggestions
  for teaching each lesson.

Sheppard, Eugenia, and Castro U., Elsa. <u>Horas Felices</u>.
  México, D.F., Editorial Patria, S.A., 1959. 126 pp.
      This book revolves around the lives of a
  group of children as they come in contact with
  their brothers, sisters, and relatives. Their relationship to school, other people, and country is
  stressed. The language of the book is appropriate
  for small children.

Vogam, Grace Dawson. <u>Let's Talk Spanish, Book I</u>. Illustrated by Phil Kantz. Skokie, Ill.: Banks Upshaw
Division, National Textbook Corp., 1962. 91 pp.
   <u>Let's Talk Spanish</u> is the first of a two-book
series written to be used in the primary grades.
It introduces the Spanish vowel sounds and through
simple stories and dialogues builds a beginning
Spanish reading and speaking vocabulary.

Grade 2

Jones, Edwina; Morgan, Edna; Landis, Paul E.; and Shaw,
Thelma. <u>Mi Primer Libro de la Salud</u>. Translated
and adapted by Angeles Pastor. River Forest, Ill.:
Laidlaw Brothers, Inc., 1959. 97 pp.
   In simple Spanish <u>Mi Primer Libro de la Salud</u>
presents stories and games which teach beginning
concepts of good nutrition, personal hygiene and
safety, the importance of medical examinations and
the need for good mental health. Colorful illus-
trations add to the attractive format of the book.
Five pages in the back of the book contain suggestions for the teacher in presenting the lessons and
games and the vocabulary used in the book.

Grades 1-3

<u>The Cat in the Hat Beginner Book Dictionary in Spanish</u>.
New York: Random House, Inc., 1966. 135 pp.
   This book is based on the original <u>Beginner
Book Dictionary</u> and was adapted into beginner's
Spanish by Robert R. Nardelli, Ph.D., Professor of
Education, San Diego State College. Words are
listed in English; colorful cartoon figures by
P. D. Eastman and a sentence in English and in
Spanish illustrate the meaning of the word. At
the end of the word list are two pages written by
Dr. Carlos Rivera, Coordinator of Spanish in the
Elementary Grades, El Paso, Texas, which explain
Spanish pronunciation of consonants and vowels,
formation of Spanish syllables and word stress and
written accent in Spanish.

Grade 2 or 3

Pastor, Angeles; Vda. de Capo, Rosa Guzmán; Tejera, Carmen
    Gómez; and Hester, Kathleen B. Pueblo y campo.
    Illustrated by Beth Wilson. River Forest, Ill.:
    Laidlaw Brothers, Inc., 1962. 192 pp.
        Pueblo y campo is the fifth book in the
    series Por el mundo de cuento y la aventura. It is
    preceded by a readiness book, two pre-primers, and
    a first level reader. This book extends the reading
    skills introduced in the first readers and helps
    the child begin to make visual and phonetic analyses
    of the words he reads. It stresses comprehension
    in oral and silent reading while providing for
    individual differences among the children through
    the practice and enrichment exercises provided in
    the teacher's manual. The book is divided into six
    topical sections with one or two review pages fol-
    lowing each section.

Grade 3

Jones, Edwina; Morgan, Edna; Landis, Paul E.; and Shaw,
    Thelma. Mi Segundo Libro de la Salud. Translated
    and adapted by Angeles Pastor. River Forest, Ill.:
    Laidlaw Brothers, Inc., 1959. 128 pp.
        Mi Segundo Libro de la Salud is the second
    book of the series El Camino Hacia la Salud. It
    extends the concepts of health introduced in Mi
    Primer Libro de la Salud and introduces information
    about communicable diseases, physical development,
    and sanitation. Eight pages in the back of the book
    contain suggestions for the teacher in the presenta-
    tion of the lessons and concepts to be developed as
    well as a vocabulary list.

Grades 1-6

Mireles, E. E., and Mireles, Jovita G. El Español Ele-
    mental. Austin: W. S. Benson & Company, 1949.
    118 pp. (Series of 6 books--Primer Libro--Sexto
    Libro).
        In this series of six elementary Spanish books,
    the commonest words are introduced first. Begin-
    ning with Primer Libro, some 1,800 of the highest
    frequency words, taken from the authoritative word
    counts, are introduced approximately in the order

of their frequencies. The total number of running words in the series is 29,500; the average repetition per word, 16.

This new series is presented with the idea of meeting the need for a complete elementary course that will furnish our pupils with the means of learning to speak, read, and write the most useful words of the Spanish language.

J. T. Brackenridge Elementary School
(San Antonio, Texas)

SAN ANTONIO BILINGUAL DEMONSTRATION
AND DISSEMINATION CENTER

Curriculum Materials Under Development and in
Pilot Test by the Southwest Educational
Development Laboratory

Science - Grade One

The oral language development in both English and Spanish utilizes the content of science adapted from the American Association for the Advancement of Science. The content is selected and organized to provide indictive approaches for the development of cognitive skills concomitantly with systematic skill development in language. The language developed in each lesson, both structure patterns and vocabulary, is determined by the content of the lesson and represents the language essential for explaining and communicating learning experiences. Five scientific processes are presented in the First Grade. They are: Observing, Space/Time Relationships, Using Numbers, Measuring, and Classifying. These processes will continue to be developed at varying degrees of depth and complexity at each grade level. The topics of study for first grade are as follows:

   I.   Two-Dimensional Shapes (15 lessons)

   II. Three-Dimensional Shapes (11 lessons)

   III. Change (solids, liquids, color, texture, sound, etc. 11 lessons)

   IV. Sets and Their Members (11 lessons)

Science - Grade Two

The science content at Grade Two is a further development of the work begun at First Grade level. As
concepts are formulated and further developed through
meaningful experiences, the structured language program
focuses attention to the language of science (in both
English and Spanish).

The eighteen units of study in the Second Grade
include the following AAAS processes: Classifying,
Observing, Communicating, Measuring, Using Space/Time
Relationships, and Using Numbers.

Science - Grade Three

The oral language development in both English and
Spanish continues to reinforce the science processes
developed in Grades One and Two. Grade Three includes
eighteen topics of study which further develop the following AAAS Processes: Classifying, Communicating, Space/
Time Relationships, Observing, Predicting, Inferring,
Measuring, and Using Numbers.

Science - Grades Four and Five

In the first three grades of the Oral Language
Science Program the child learns the cognitive skills and
behaviors associated with this approach and the linguistic
symbolization for these experiences. The scientific
processes developed have been previously listed. In Grade
Four beyond, these processes are presented with added
depth and integrated with the following: Defining Opera-
tionally, Controlling Variables, Experimenting, Formulating
Models, Interpreting Data. All the experiences are
accompanied by appropriate language buildup in order that
the child may verbalize and communicate his understanding
to others.

There are thirteen lessons on Fourth Grade level
and twelve lessons on Fifth Grade level.

Social Studies - Grades One, Two, and Three

Through the Social Studies Language Development
Program, in both English and Spanish, the children are provided a conceptual base from which future learnings can

grow; it is from this conceptual base that meaningful
language emerges. Thus, this program provides for growth
in meanings and in the symbols expressing them.

The thirty-one topics of study in the First Grade,
the fifteen topics in the Second Grade, and the eighteen
topics in the Third Grade can be broken down into the
following major concepts:

I.   How Do We Live?

II.   Where Do We Live?

III. What Are We Like?

IV.   How Do We Make A Living?

V.   How Are We Governed?

VI.   What Have We Done?

VII. How Do We Express Ourselves?

Self-Concept - Grade One

The objectives of these lessons are: developing a
sense of personal identity, acquiring experiences in a
social context, and developing cognitive patterns--all
important to successful academic learning.

The development of oral language communication in
the social setting is generally focused upon two aspects,
differentiating oneself from others and perceiving oneself as a member of various groups. The specific focus
is upon: (1) teaching the child to understand and express
essential information about himself and his personal needs,
and (2) learning the routines and directions for group
work in a classroom. Through Levels I and II, the ground-
work for several basic concepts will be developed--self,
family, school.

Level I - The Child and His World (10 lessons)

Level II - The Senses (9 lessons)

Oral and Written Composition

Most teachers at present tend to teach writing
skills through extensive free practice based on corrected

errors after they are made rather than before. This handbook suggests an effective writing program which will make
it possible for children with a language deficiency to
write papers that are comparatively free of errors from the
very first efforts. The various skills are presented in
orderly sequences.

The Teachers' Handbook contains the following:

    1. Readiness and Beginning Handwriting
    2. Handwriting
    3. Written Communication: The First Grade
    4. Spelling
    5. Composition by Pattern Writing
    6. From Thoughts to Written Words
    7. Functional Writing
    8. Some Ideas for Creative Composition, Grades 2,
        3, 4, 5.
    9. Paragraph Writing
  10. Poetic Expression
  11. Haiku

Reading Development Series

    Shape Books, Grade 1 (includes eighteen books--
nine each in English and Spanish). A reading program
based on the oral language experiences which the children
have had.

Nye Elementary School
(Laredo, Texas)

Blyton, Enid. Un Susto Para Los Siete Secretos. Bar-
    celona, Spain: Editorial Juventud, S.A., 1964.
        A storybook in translation. Original title:
    Shock for the Secret Seven.

Brady, Agnes M. Mi Libro de Español. Illustrated by
    Bergen-Patterson. Columbus, Ohio: Charles E.
    Merrill Books, Inc., 1956.
        One of the better texts for FLES and for the
    bilingual program which has need for an hour block
    time devoted to the study of Spanish. Content
    logically arranged, good vocabulary, not watered
    down. Contains the following areas of study:
    Lecciones de Geografía, Lecturas, Anciones, Buen
    Provecho, Adivinanzas, Refranes, Trabalenguas,
    Spanish-English Dictionary.

Cebollero, Pedro A., and Haydon, Rosa Navarro. <u>La Ciencia</u>
    <u>en Nuestra Vida</u>. Illustrated by Pru Herric.
    Boston: Ginn and Company, 1957.
        Edited in collaboration with the Department
of Public Instruction, Puerto Rico. A well-
illustrated book of elementary science with authentic scientific vocabulary. Table of Contents:
Cambios que ocurren en el cielo; El Aire, El
Viento, y el Huracán; Las Plantas que no dan
semillas; La Hoja verde es una fábrica; Animales
sin espinazo; El agricultor utiliza la ciencia,
etc.

       . <u>Aire y Sol</u>. Illustrated by Pru Herric. Boston:
    Ginn and Company, 1956.
        An elementary book for science. Appropriate
vocabulary. Sample Units: cosas con vida y cosas
sin vida, como viven los animales y las plantas,
animales con espinazo, las plantas que dan semillas,
plantas del mar a la montana, etc.

Schmitt, Conrad J. <u>Let's Speak Spanish 4</u>. Illustrated by
    Tom Lavelle and Associates. St. Louis: McGraw-
    Hill Book Company, 1964.
        <u>Let's Speak Spanish 4</u> provides the third
dimension in this sequential audio-lingual-visual
program. The text continues and expands listening,
speaking, and reading skills and introduces writing.
        All reading selections are culturally oriented
to the Hispanic worlds.
        Every unit is accompanied by a test. Some
units require the students to have their books open
during the test so that they may refer to pictures
which are described on the disk recordings. An
attractive book.

Seuss, Dr. <u>The Cat in the Hat</u> (<u>El Gato Ensombrerado</u>).
    Translated by Carlos Rivera. New York: Random
    House, 1956.
        A children's storybook with English-Spanish
on the same page. Beautifully illustrated. A
beginner's book.

Coral Way Elementary School
(Miami, Florida)

English as a Second Language:

American English Series, Books 1-2. Revised edition of
Fries American English Series. Boston: D. C.
Heath and Co.

English for Today, Books 1-3. New York: McGraw-Hill
Book Company.

Fries American English Series, Books 1-4. Boston:
D. C. Heath and Co.

Miami Linguistic Readers. Boston: D. C. Heath and Co.

Health:

El Camino Hacia la Salud, Books 1-6. River Forest,
Ill.: Laidlaw Brothers, Inc.

Language:

Almendros-Alvero. Lengua Española, Libros 1-6.
Guatemala, Guatemala: Cultural Centroamericana,
S.A.

Mathematics:

Roca, Pablo (trans.). Matematica Moderna (Books 1-2).
Atlanta, Georgia: Silver Burdett and Co.

Reading:

Por el Mundo del Cuento y la Aventura (Readiness-Book
VI). River Forest, Ill.: Laidlaw Brothers, Inc.

Science:

Fresquet, Alberto E. J. Elementos de Ciencias Natur-
ales (7th-8th Grades). Buenos Aires, Argentina:
Editorial Kapelusz.

La Ciencia, Books 1-4 (5-6 in preparation). Boston:
D. C. Heath and Co.

Rodriquez, Elio Arrechea. Nuestro Mundo, Libros I-VI.
Caracas, Venezuela: Cultural Venezolana, S.A.

Social Studies:

Marrero, Levi. Viajemos por America (5th Grade).
    Caracas, Venezuela: Cultural Venezolana, S.A.

    _____. Viajemos por el Mundo (6th Grade). Caracas,
    Venezuela: Cultural Venezolana, S.A.

América de Todos (7th-8th Grades). Chicago, Ill.:
    Rand McNally and Company.

Passadori, Josefina. Elementos de Geografía (7th-
    8th Grades). Buenos Aires, Argentina: Editorial
    Kapelusz.

Spanish for Spanish-Speaking Pupils:

Por el Mundo del Cuento y la Aventura, Pre-Primer--
    Book V. River Forest, Ill.: Laidlaw Brothers,
    Inc.

Almendros-Alvero. Lengua Espanola, Libros 1-5.
    Guatemala, Guatemala: Cultural Centroamericana,
    S.A.

APPENDIX D

QUESTIONNAIRE FOR SUPERVISORS OR DIRECTORS OF

BILINGUAL EDUCATION PROGRAMS FOR

THE SPANISH-SPEAKING CHILD

Part I. General Information. Please answer all questions.
Many questions may be answered by check mark ( )
or fill-in; others invite comment on practices
you may have discovered and believe to be valuable (more space on back if needed).

1. In what kind of community is your school located and
what type of student does it serve?

Total School Enrollment _____ Ethnic Composition:

2. How do you classify your bilingual program?

____ A. A program _for_ bilinguals. This type of program
is _for_ bilinguals; the program itself is not bilingual. It has a strong ESL (English as a
Second Language) component.

____ B. A "bridge" program. The purpose of this program
is definitely the preparation of the student to
enter the English curriculum as soon as possible.

____ C. A "real" bilingual program. This type of program
is one in which two languages (English and Spanish) are used as the mediums of instruction for
any part or all of the curriculum. Bilingualism
and biculturalism are the desired goals at the
end of the elementary school program.

3. Objectives. Please outline, briefly, the stated
objectives of your bilingual education program. If
you have a prepared statement of these objectives,
please attach to this questionnaire.

162

4. Time and Treatment of the bilingual program curriculum.

   A. Indicate the per cent of class time devoted to
       English and Spanish by grade level:

	1	2	3	4	5	6
English	___	___	___	___	___	___
Spanish	___	___	___	___	___	___

   B. Indicate with a check mark ( ) if instruction
       in Spanish is given in the following elementary
       school curriculum:

	Spanish Class	Social Studies	Math	Science	Music	Physical Education	
Language							
Cultural Information							
Subject Matter							

   C. Placement Procedure. Do you have placement pro-
       cedures to place students in the bilingual
       program?

                                   (yes)   (no)

       If yes, what is the basis for placement in the
       bilingual program?

       _____ Tests
       _____ Educational Background
       _____ Pupil Choice
       _____ Other Means

       Comments:

D. Articulation.

    1. Extent of the bilingual program: ____ 1-6
                                            ____ 1-9
                                            Other
                                            (indicate)

    2. Extent of Articulation: ____ 1-6
                                   ____ 1-9
                                   Other
                                   (indicate)

    3. Is the program articulated for:

                               ____ non-English speakers
                               ____ non-Spanish speakers
                               ____ bilinguals

    4. Does the articulated program meet the needs
        of the
                               ____ non-English speakers
                               ____ non-Spanish speakers
                               ____ bilinguals

5. Teaching Strategies.

    A. Classroom Strategies. Check the procedures that
        apply in your bilingual program:

        ____ lecture   ____ FLES (Foreign Lan-
        ____ group discussion   guage in the
        ____ team teaching   Elementary School)
        ____ individual study   ____ ESL (English as a
        ____ library assignment   Second Language)
        ____ other (indicate)   ____ Spanish for the
        ____   Spanish-Speaking
                                         ____ other (indicate)
                                         ____

    B. Radio and Television.

        1. Are radio and television being used in the
            bilingual program?
                                     (yes) (no)
            Which medium?   ____ radio
                                       ____ TV
                                       ____ both

        2. What language is being used?
                                     ____ Spanish
                                     ____ English
                                     ____ both

3. How is the media used?
- _____ for basic presentation
- _____ for enrichment
- _____ both

4. For what purpose is the media used?
- _____ language instruction
- _____ culture presentation
- _____ general knowledge

5. Use of other media:
- _____ language laboratory
- _____ newspaper
- _____ magazine
- _____ other (indicate)

_____ _____

_____ _____

Comments:

C. Extra-Curricular Activities. Check the activities that apply to your bilingual program:

1. School-related
- _____ Clubs
- _____ Language Week
- _____ Extra Lab Use
- _____ Preparation of Posters
- _____ Class Projects

2. Out-of-School
- _____ Pen Pals
- _____ Student Exchange
- _____ other (indicate)

_____ _____

_____ _____

6. Acculturation (Ethnic Group Identification, Self-Image)

A. Culture: Strong ethnic identification _____
                 Weak ethnic identification _____
                 Strong bicultural ident-
                 ification _____
                 Weak bicultural identifica-
                 tion _____

B. Language: Much importance on Spanish ____
                      Some importance on Spanish ____
                      Little importance on Spanish ____

C. Foreign language (Spanish) reflects:
                      Mexican culture   ____
                      Mexican-American culture   ____
                      Spanish culture   ____
                      Puerto Rican culture   ____
                      Puerto Rican-American cul-
                      ture   ____
                      Cuban culture   ____
                      Cuban-American culture   ____

Part II. Staff and Teacher Education.

1. Teaching, Supportive, and Administrative Staff. Please
    check the appropriate blanks.

A.   Language Command   Program Support

ADMINISTRATIVE		Total Number	English	Spanish	English-Spanish (Bilinguals)	Strong	Moderate	Weak	Does Not Support
	Superintendent								
	Principal								
	Supervisor								
	Visiting Teacher								

B.

	Language Command				Program Support			
T E A C H I N G	Total Number	English	Spanish	English-Spanish (Bilinguals)	Strong	Moderate	Weak	Does Not Support
Anglo								
Latin American								

C.

S U P P O R T I V E								
Counselors								
a. Guidance								
b. Psychologist								
Nurse								
Librarian								
Aides								
Cooks								
Janitors								
Secretary								
Clerk								
Other								

Bilingual teachers educated in: Latin America or
Spain   ____

United States   ____

Elsewhere   ____

2.   In-Service Training for Teachers in Bilingual Programs.

Type	Desired Goal				Cultural Development						Utilization		
	Self-Improvement	Proficiency in Language Usage	Proficiency in Related Methodology	(Other)	As a Person	As a Member of an Ethnic Group	As a Citizen	In Basic Cultural Knowledge	Method of Teaching Culture	(Other)	As Public Speakers for Ethnic Group	As Advisors by School Agencies	(Other)
Local													
System-wide													

3.   College and University Training in the Immediate Area
      of the Bilingual School.

                                              yes   no
                        Available   ___   ___
                        EPDA Institute   ___   ___
                        Special Institute   ___   ___

      (If special institute, explain below.)

4.   Study Abroad Requirement for Teachers in Bilingual
      Program.

                                      required   ___
                        not required   ___
                            encouraged   ___
                    not encouraged   ___
        neither required nor encouraged   ___

5.   Pre-Service Training for Prospective Teachers for
      Bilingual Programs.

                        Available
                                          ‾‾‾‾‾‾   ‾‾‾‾
                                          (yes)   (no)

      (If yes, please explain below.)

Part III.   Evaluation of Bilingual Program:

                        provided for   _____
                        not provided for   _____
                        on-going   _____
                        not on-going   _____
                        limited   _____

      (If limited, please explain.)

      Are Achievement Results being kept?
                                          ‾‾‾‾‾‾   ‾‾‾‾
                                          (yes)   (no)

      (If yes, please comment below on your interpretation
      of these achievement results.)

Part IV.   Community Involvement.

1.   Parent Participation.   Parents help children with:

                                          (yes)   (no)
                        oral practice   _____ _____
                        reading   _____ _____
                        writing   _____ _____
            (other)   _____   _____ _____

                        _____   _____ _____

2.   Community Workers Support the Bilingual Program by:

            Worker   Service Rendered

Professional _____   _____
Trades   _____   _____
Business   _____   _____

Worker	Service Rendered

Manual
Farming

3. Vocational Agencies that Support the Bilingual
    Program.

Name	Service Rendered

4. Social Agencies that Support the Bilingual Program.

Name	Service Rendered

Part V. Comments and Conclusions.

1. What do you consider to be the strongest and the
    weakest points in your bilingual program?

    a) The Strongest Point:

    b) The Weakest Point:

2. Please give your comments on the conclusions that you
    have come to in regard to your bilingual program:
    (Use back side of page if necessary.)

Part VI.   Instructional Materials and Library Services.

1.   Materials.   Are your materials:

            _____ Self-made (teacher-made)
            _____ Commercial
            _____ Created specifically for your
                  local area by the school
                  system
            _____ Experimental

    Please submit a bibliography of your instructional
    materials by grade level and subject matter.   Perhaps
    you have an annotated bibliography which you may sub-
    mit.

2.   Library.

      A.   Type of Books.
           Give the approximate number of books in:

                  _____ Spanish Language
                  _____ English Language
                  _____ English-Spanish

      B.   Library Instruction.

           1. Story Telling
                  _____ in Spanish
                  _____ in English
                  _____ in both languages

           2. On use of library
                  _____ in Spanish
                  _____ in English
                  _____ in both languages

           3. Supplementary Aids
                  _____ Spanish filmstrips
                  _____ Spanish tape recording
                  _____ Spanish transparencies
                  _____ Spanish Grammar Stencils
                        (commercial)

COMMENTS. Please give your comments (on items not covered
           above, or covered above).

           a)   Covered above:

           b)   Not Covered above:

Additional Comments:

BIBLIOGRAPHY

BIBLIOGRAPHY

Books and Pamphlets

Axelrod, Joseph. The Education of the Modern Foreign Language Teacher for American Schools. The Modern Language Association of America, 1966.

Brooks, Nelson. Language and Language Learning. New York: Harcourt Brace and World, Inc., 1960.

Haselden, Kyle. Death of a Myth. New York: Friendship Press, 1964.

Heller, Celia S. Mexican-American Youth: Forgotten Youth at Crossroads. New York: Random House, 1966.

Kline, Otto, and Lambert, Wallace E. Children's Views of Foreign Peoples. New York: Appleton-Century-Crofts, 1967.

Lado, Robert. Language Teaching: A Scientific Approach. New York: McGraw-Hill Book Company, Inc., 1966.

Southeastern Education Laboratory. Razon de Ser of the Bilingual School. Atlanta, Georgia: Southeastern Education Laboratory.

Valdman, Albert, ed. Trends in Language Teaching. New York: McGraw-Hill Book Company, Inc., 1966.

Professional Reports and Government Legislation

Bilingual Education Act. Title VII of the Elementary and Secondary Education Act Amendments of 1967, P.L. 90-247.

Del Rio Independent School District. Evaluation of the Garfield Experimental Program in Bilingual Education. Del Rio, Texas: Del Rio Independent School District, September 27, 1968.

Elementary and Secondary Education Act Amendment of 1967, Title VII. Bilingual Education Act. P.L. 90-247.

Fishman, Joshua A.; Cooper, Robert L.; Ma, Roxana; et al. Bilingualism in the Barrio. Final Report: Yeshiva University, Contract No. OEC-7-062817-0297, U.S. Department of Health, Education and Welfare, 1968. Washington, D.C.: Department of Health, Education and Welfare, 1968.

NEA-Tucson Survey. The Invisible Minority. Washington, D.C.: National Education Association, 1966.

Reports of the Working Committees. Foreign Language Teaching: Challenges to the Profession. The Northeast Conference on the Teaching of Foreign Languages, 1965.

Southwest Council of Foreign Language Teachers. Reports: Our Bilinguals. El Paso, Texas, 1965.

_____. Reports: Bilingualism. El Paso, Texas, 1966.

_____. Reports: Bilingual Education. El Paso, Texas, 1967.

_____. Reports: Bilingual Education in Three Cultures. El Paso, Texas, 1968.

Southwest Educational Development Laboratory. Education and Social Change. Austin, Texas, 1967.

_____. National Conference on Educational Opportunities for Mexican-Americans, April 25-26, 1968, Austin, Texas.

_____. Texas Conference for the Mexican-American, April 13-15, 1967, San Antonio, Texas.

Texas Education Agency. Conference on Development of Bilingualism in Children of Varying Linguistic and Cultural Heritages. Addresses and Reports. Austin, Texas: Texas Education Agency, January 31, 1967.

U.S. Senate. Committee on Labor and Public Welfare. Hearings Before the Special Subcommittee on Bilingual Education, Part 1, 90th Cong., 1st Sess., 1967.

U.S. Senate. Committee on Labor and Public Welfare. <u>Hear-</u>
<u>ings Before the Special Subcommittee on Bilingual</u>
<u>Education</u>, Part II, 90th Cong., 1st Sess., 1967.

Journals and Periodicals

Adkins, Patricia. "Teaching Idioms and Figures of Speech
to Non-Native Speakers of English." <u>Modern Lan-</u>
<u>guage Journal</u>, LII (March, 1968), 148-152.

Andersson, Theodore. "Bilingual Schooling: Oasis or
Mirage?" <u>Hispania</u>, LII (March, 1969), 69-74.

_____. "A New Focus on the Bilingual Child." <u>Modern</u>
<u>Language Journal</u>, XLIX (March, 1965), 156-160.

Belasco, Simon. "Toward the Acquisition of Linguistic
Competence: From Contrived to Controlled Material."
<u>Modern Language Journal</u>, LII (March, 1969), 185-205.

Bendiner, Elmer. "Outside the Kingdom of the Middle
Class." <u>The Nation</u>, CCIV (January 2, 1967), 22-23.

Berney, Tomi D., and Cooper, Robert L. "Semantic Independence and Degree of Bilingualism in Two Communities." <u>Modern Language Journal</u>, LIII (March,
1969), 182-185.

Boyer, Mildred. "Bilingual Schooling: A Dimension of
Democracy." Texas Foreign Language Association
<u>Bulletin</u>, II (December, 1968), 1-6.

Brooks, Nelson. "The Meaning of Bilingualism Today."
<u>Foreign Language Annals</u>, II (March, 1969), 304-309.

Bus, Dan. "The Bi-Lingual Approach: Del Rio Technique."
<u>Del Rio News-Herald</u> (Texas), March 23, 1969, Sec-
tion B, 1-2.

Christian, Chester. "The Acculturation of the Bilingual
Child." <u>Modern Language Journal</u>, XLIX (March,
1965), 160-165.

"Commonwealth of Puerto Rico." <u>Encyclopedia Americana</u>,
XXII (1969).

Cooper, Robert L. "Two Contextualized Measures of Degree of Bilingualism." Modern Language Journal, LIII (March, 1969), 172-178.

_____, and Greenfield, Lawrence. "Language Use in a Bilingual Community." Modern Language Journal, LIII (March, 1969), 166-172.

_____. "Word Frequency Estimation as a Measure of Degree of Bilingualism." Modern Language Journal, LIII (March, 1969), 163-166.

Donoghue, Mildred. "A Rationale for FLES." French Review, XXXVIII (February, 1965), 523-529.

Edelman, Martin. "The Contextualization of Schoolchildren's Bilingualism." Modern Language Journal, LIII (March, 1969), 179-182.

Fishman, Joshua A., and Casiano, Heriberto. "Puerto Ricans in Our Press." Modern Language Journal, LIII (March, 1969), 157-162.

Fishman, Joshua A. "The Status and Prospects of Bilingualism in the United States." Modern Language Journal, XLIX (March, 1965), 143-155.

_____. "The Measurement and Description of Widespread and Relatively Stable Bilingualism." Modern Language Journal, LIII (March, 1969), 152-156.

Fish, Sherrill. "What Goals for FLES?" Hispania, LII (March, 1969), 64-69.

Florida Foreign Language Reporter. Editorial, January, 1965.

Gaarder, A. Bruce. "Teaching the Bilingual Child: Research, Development, and Policy." Modern Language Journal, XLIX (March, 1965), 160-175.

_____. "Organization of the Bilingual School." The Journal of Social Issues, XXXIII (April, 1967), 110-120.

González, Josue M. "Bilingual Program Involves 4,000 Students." San Antonio Independent School District Our Schools, XXI (November, 1968), 2-3.

Howe, Harold, II. "Cowboys, Indians, and American Educa-
    tion." The Texas Outlook, LII (June, 1968), 13-25.

Hubbard, Louise J. "Modern Foreign Languages for the
    Racially Disadvantaged." Modern Language Journal,
    LII (March, 1968), 139-140.

Ibarra, Herbert. "Teaching Spanish to the Spanish-
    Speaking." Foreign Language Annals, II (March,
    1969), 310-315.

Lewis, Glyn E. "Language and Language Development."
    Bilingualism in the Schools of Wales. Swansea,
    Wales: Welsh Department, Ministry of Education,
    University College (January, 1962), 9-16.

Perales, Alonso M. "The Audio-Lingual Approach and the
    Spanish-Speaking Student." Hispania, XLVIII (March,
    1965), 99-102.

Rojas, Pauline M. "Instructional Materials and Aids to
    Facilitate Teaching the Bilingual Child." Modern
    Language Journal, XLIX (February, 1965), 237-240.

Soriano, Jesse M., and McClafferty, James. "Spanish
    Speakers of the Midwest: They are Americans, Too."
    Foreign Language Annals, II (March, 1969), 316-324.

Ury, Claude M. "The Bilingual Education Act--Bridge to
    Understanding." The Catholic School Journal,
    LXVIII (September, 1968), 33-35.

Vogeley, Nancy. "The Challenge to Foreign Language Teach-
    ing Presented by the Disadvantaged." Hispania,
    XLIX (December, 1966), 813-817.

Walk, Elsie. "The Teaching of English as a Second Lan-
    guage in the Elementary Schools of New York City."
    Hispania, XLIX (May, 1966), 293-296.

Walsh, Donald D. "Bilingualism and Bilingual Education:
    A Guest Editorial." Foreign Language Annals, II
    (March, 1969), 298-303.

_____. "Longer and Better: The Foreign Language
    Sequence." Modern Language Journal, LII (November,
    1968), 424-431.

_____. "Too Little and Too Late." Modern Language
    Journal, XLIX (March, 1965), 83.

Wonder, John P. "The Bilingual Mexican-American as a
    Potential Teacher of Spanish." Hispania, XLVIII
    (March, 1965), 97-99.

Yarborough, Ralph W. "Bilingual Education as a Social
    Force." Foreign Language Annals, II (March, 1969),
    325-327.

Research Reports

Cheavens, Sam Frank. "Vernacular Languages and Education."
    Unpublished Ph.D. dissertation, The University of
    Texas, 1957.

Logan, J. Lee. "Recommendations for Planning a Bilingual
    Program." Part of a paper presented to The Confer-
    ence on Conservation of Bilingual Resources at the
    University of Michigan, Ann Arbor, March 18, 1967.

Murphy, Joseph A. "The Contributions of Social Studies
    Methodology to Foreign Language Teaching." Unpub-
    lished Ph.D. dissertation, The Ohio State Univer-
    sity, 1968.

Raisner, Arnold D.; Bolger, Philip A.; and Sanguinetti,
    Carmen. Science Instruction in Spanish for Pupils
    of Spanish-Speaking Background. Bureau of Educa-
    tional Research, Board of Education of the City of
    New York, 1967.

Richardson, Mabel Wilson. "An Evaluation of Certain
    Aspects of the Academic Achievement of Elementary
    Pupils in a Bilingual Program." Unpublished Ph.D.
    dissertation, The University of Miami, 1968.

Slominski, Carmen. "The Relationship of Bilingualism to
    School Achievement." Unpublished seminar report,
    The Ohio State University, 1968.

Treviño, Bertha. "An Analysis of the Effectiveness of a
    Bilingual Program in the Teaching of Mathematics
    in the Primary Grades." Unpublished Ph.D. dis-
    sertation, The University of Texas at Austin, 1968.

Correspondence, Lectures, and
Personal Communications

Andersson, Theodore. Director, USOE Bilingual Design, Southwest Educational Development Laboratory, Austin, Texas. Letter of February 28, 1969.

Brantley, Harold. Superintendent, United Consolidated Independent School District, Laredo, Texas. Personal interview, March 10, 1969.

Peña, Albar. Program Advisor, Bilingual Education Section, U.S. Office of Education, Washington, D.C. Telephone interview, March 5, 1969.

Peña, Albar. Program Advisor, Bilingual Education Section, U.S. Office of Education, Washington, D.C. Telephone interview, April 29, 1969.

Rodríguez, Armando. Chief, Mexican-American Affairs Unit, U.S. Office of Education, Washington, D.C. Telephone interview, March 5, 1969.

Rodríguez, Armando. Chief, Mexican-American Affairs Unit, U.S. Office of Education, Washington, D.C. Letter of July 12, 1968.

BILINGUAL-BICULTURAL EDUCATION IN THE UNITED STATES

An Arno Press Collection

Allen, Harold B. **A Survey of the Teaching of English to Non-English Speakers in the United States.** 1966

Allen, Virginia F. and Sidney Forman. **English As A Second Language.** [1967]

Aucamp, A.J. **Bilingual Education and Nationalism With Special Reference to South Africa.** 1926

Axelrod, Herman C. **Bilingual Background And Its Relation to Certain Aspects of Character and Personality of Elementary School Children** (Doctoral Dissertation, Yeshiva University, 1951). 1978

Bengelsdorf, Winnie. **Cthnic Studies in Higher Education.** 1972

Berrol, Selma Cantor. **Immigrants at School: New York City** (Doctoral Dissertation, City University of New York, 1967). 1978

Cordasco, Francesco, ed. **Bilingualism and the Bilingual Child.** 1978

Cordasco, Francesco, ed. **The Bilingual-Bicultural Child and the Question of   Intelligence.** 1978

Cordasco, Francesco, ed. **Bilingual Education in New York City.** 1978

Dissemination Center for Bilingual Bicultural Education. **Guide to Title VII ESEA Bilingual Bicultural Projects, 1973-1974.** 1974

Dissemination Center for Bilingual Bicultural Education. **Proceedings, National Conference on Bilingual Education.** 1975

Fishman, Joshua A. **Language Loyalty in the United States.** 1966

Flores, Solomon Hernández. **The Nature and Effectiveness of Bilingual Education Programs for the Spanish-Speaking Child in the United States** (Doctoral Dissertation, Ohio State University, 1969). 1978

Galvan, Robert Rogers. **Bilingualism As It Relates to Intelligence Test Scores and School Achievement Among Culturally Deprived Spanish-American Children** (Doctoral Dissertation, East Texas State University, 1967). 1978

Illinois State Advisory Committee. **Bilingual/Bicultural Education.** 1974

Levy, Rosemary Salomone. **An Analysis of the Effects of Language Acquisition Context Upon the Dual Language Development of Non-English Dominant Students** (Doctoral Dissertation, Columbia University, 1976). 1978

Malherbe, Ernst G. **The Bilingual School.** 1946

Mandera, Franklin Richard. **An Inquiry into the Effects of Bilingualism on Native and Non-Native Americans** (Doctoral Dissertation, University of Illinois, 1971). 1978

Materials and Human Resources for Teaching Ethnic Studies. 1975

Medina, Amelia Cirilo. **A Comparative Analysis of Evaluative Theory and Practice for the Instructional Component of Bilingual Programs** Doctoral Dissertation, Texas A&M University, 1975). 1978

National Advisory Council on Bilingual Education. **Bilingual Education.** 1975

Peebles, Robert Whitney. **Leonard Covello: A Study of an Immigrant's Contribution to New York City** (Doctoral Dissertation, New York University, 1967). 1978

Reyes, Vinicio H. **Bicultural-Bilingual Education for Latino Students** (Doctoral Dissertation, University of Massachusetts, 1975). 1978

Rodriguez M[unguia], Juan C. **Supervision of Bilingual Programs** (Doctoral Dissertation, Loyola University of Chicago, 1974). 1978

Royal Commission on Bilingualism and Biculturalism. **Preliminary Report and Books I & II.** 3 vols. in 1. 1965/1967/1968

Streiff, Paul Robert. **Development of Guidelines for Conducting Research in Bilingual Education** (Doctoral Dissertation, University of California, Los Angeles, 1974). 1978

Streiff, Virginia. **Reading Comprehension and Language Proficiency Among Eskimo Children** (Doctoral Dissertation, Ohio University, 1977). 1978

Ulibarri, Horatio. **Interpretative Studies on Bilingual Education.** 1969

United Kingdom, Department of Education and Science, National Commission for Unesco. **Bilingualism in Education.** 1965

United Nations Educational Scientific and Cultural Organization. **The Use of Vernacular Languages in Education.** 1953

United States Bureau of Indian Affairs. **Bilingual Education for American Indians.** 1971

United States Commission on Civil Rights. **Mexican American Education Study.** 5 vols. in 1. 1971-1973

United States House of Representatives. **Bilingual Education Programs.** 1967

United States House of Representatives. **United States Ethnic Heritage Studies Centers.** 1970

United States Senate. **Bilingual Education, Health, and Manpower Programs.** 1973

United States. Senate. **Bilingual Education, Hearings.** 1967

Viereck, Louis. **German Instruction in American Schools.** 1902